W9-CDX-364

$ 28.03

InfoThink

InfoThink

Practical Strategies for Using Information in Business

Mary Woodfill Park

The Scarecrow Press, Inc.
Lanham, Md., & London
1998

SCARECROW PRESS, INC.

Published in the United States of America
by Scarecrow Press, Inc.
4720 Boston Way
Lanham, Maryland 20706

4 Pleydell Gardens, Folkestone
Kent CT20 2DN, England

British Library Cataloguing in Publication Information Available

Library of Congress Cataloging-in-Publication Data

Park, Mary Woodfill.
     InfoThink : practical strategies for using information in
  business / Mary Woodfill Park.
        p.   cm.
     Includes bibliographical references and index.
     ISBN 0-8108-3424-3 (cloth : alk. paper)
     1. Management information systems. 2. Management—Information
  services. I. Title.
HD30.213.P36 1998
658.4'038—DC21   97-42346

ISBN 0-8108-3424-3 (cloth : alk. paper)

♾™ The paper used in this publication meets the minimum requirements of American National Standard for Information Sciences—Permanence of Paper for Printed Library Materials, ANSI Z39.48–1984.
Manufactured in the United States of America.

To Lee Crandall Park, my husband, mentor, and friend who teaches me so much about so many things and who encouraged me to write this book.

Contents

PART 2: Information Professionals and Practitioners

PART 3: Information Educators and Pioneers

Figures and Tables

Foreword

Mary Park has provided the reader with a refreshing review on a personal level of those who use information on a daily basis, those who provide information to others as a part of their work, and those who manage and lead others to sources of information as well as new ways of thinking about the information profession.

The first one hundred pages of *InfoThink* are very important to those who manage and use information resources. Seven consumers of information discuss, through interviews, how they use and find information in specialized business environments. All too often, in my opinion, information managers think they know what their customers want, but really do not know. For example, the chapter on business intelligence focuses on the action orientation of U.S. executives and the need for competitive intelligence and is full of insights into methods of gathering information. This is exactly the kind of information students and practitioners should know about applications of these specialized sources and services.

Part 2 contains insights from experienced information professionals. I am particularly partial to the thoughts and thinking of Guy St. Clair, one of the interviewees in this segment of *InfoThink*. While I am forced to agree with St. Clair's use of an information audit and the necessity of tying information services to business success, I think the concept of knowledge management as the "third realm" (p. 189) of information services should open up a thought-provoking discussion for end users and practitioners.

Park's final four interviews with leaders in the library services and with thought leaders in the information industry and library and information science education were particularly well chosen, and the author has brought out the best in each.

After reading this book, I felt refreshed and, yes, even smarter than when I started. I read this book in manuscript form while on vacation. I actually felt that I had completed a two-day continuing education course that will help me think more clearly about important Information Age issues and trends.

James M. Matarazzo
Dean & Professor
Simmons College
Graduate School of Library and
Information Science

Preface

When I was young, my father and brother took me bird hunting. We walked over a gently rolling Midwest prairie, and I helped them spot the birds. I believe that thrill of the hunt experience is embedded in my psyche. The sense of anticipation and the challenge of looking for and finding something unknown carried through into my professional life, where I have become an information hunter-gatherer in the Information Age.

Most of my life I have worked with knowledgeable people in information-driven environments: in school, academic, public and corporate libraries with information professionals (also known as librarians); in the field of investments with Wall Street analysts; and in business research with information specialists. I have been exposed to the full spectrum of the information process—locating, retrieving, organizing, communicating, analyzing, and providing information for a variety of users.

I first became inspired to investigate the prospects of starting my own fee-based business research service in 1983 while I was working in the field of investments and attended a seminar in New York sponsored by the Information Industry Association, "Wall Street Meets the Information Industry." These were considered the early days of the Information Age, and it was there I heard that there would be a computer on every desk and that computers could make it possible to access information electronically—without going to the library. I saw demonstrations of powerful commercial electronic database systems, such as LEXIS-NEXIS, Dow Jones News Retrieval, and DIALOG®, that contained millions of "bits and bytes"—new terms then—of information in business and science.

By 1987, I had started my own business as an information entrepreneur, specializing in providing customized print and electronic information—"to help business make better decisions by being well-informed," my brochure said.

Since then, I have spent much of my life working and negotiating in cyberspace (I still go to libraries), and solving problems for those who are given incorrect, too much, or not enough information.

After owning and operating a business research service for seven years, I decided to write a book that would provide anecdotal, real-life stories about the many facets of using information in business with the hope that it would help people better understand and deal with the complexities of the information process in current business environments.

My methodology was to conduct personal interviews with three groups I defined as executive users of information, information professionals and practitioners, and information educators and pioneers. The resulting narratives express the thoughts of each group about the important aspects of information in their work. Please note that *InfoThink* is not to be read for a lengthy analysis or as a compendium of Internet resources, although interviewees do provide references to resources in their specific fields. More importantly, it should be read for their personal and professional insights and strategies for using and retrieving information, and for their thoughts, comments, and experiences about the important issues and technologies currently shaping their specialized uses of information, which, when combined, become *their* infothink.

Mary Woodfill Park

Acknowledgments

To those who provided support, sustenance, and encouragement to write this book:

Lee Crandall Park, Scott K. Banerjee, Stephen K. Banerjee, Alice Crandall Park, Chris Dobson, Carol and Russell Hicks, Patricia Cook, Marye Thorpe, Barbara M. Spiegelman, Ron Buchan, Mildred S. Myers, James Matarazzo, Colin McQuillan, Ann Razgunas, Pauline Bell, Karen Servary, and Vince (our cat).

Thank you to the interviewees, who shared their time, knowledge, and information experiences.

And a special thanks to my editorial advisor, Marilyn Mattsson, whose knowledge, wisdom, and good humor were key to the publication of this book, and to Eloise Liberty, editorial assistant par excellence.

M.W.P.

Introduction

There exists no human activity, and certainly no economic activity,
which directly or indirectly does not have an information component...The concepts people have in their heads, and the quality of
information available to them, determines the success or failure of an
enterprise. Knowhow is the limiting factor in wealth creation.

Tom Stonier, *The Wealth of Information: A Profile of
the Post Industrial Society*, 1983

The Current Information
Environment in Business

Peter Drucker, considered the father of modern management theory
and practice, said in his seminal 1993 *Post-Capitalist Society* that he
coined the terms "knowledge work" and "knowledge worker" around
1960, ten years after the "post-capitalist" society began.[1]

> The leading social groups of the knowledge society will
> be "knowledge workers"—knowledge executives who
> know how to allocate knowledge to productive use, just
> as the capitalists knew how to allocate capital to
> productive use; knowledge professionals; knowledge
> employees...The *economic* challenge of the post-capitalist
> society will therefore be the productivity of knowledge
> work and the knowledge worker.[2]

1

If the transition from a manufacturing society to Drucker's post-capitalist knowledge society began in the late 1940s or early 1950s, one might assume that in the late 1990s there should exist communities of practitioners well versed in all of the skills and resources required of a knowledge society, such as retrieving and using information to solve problems. Yet with the 21st century now upon us, there are signs of a movement toward information chaos in every domain—business, science, and education. And, as with Chaos Theory, it is becoming impossible to know enough at any point to predict a future state of the system. "We have more and more information coming at us, but we can't absorb it any faster than we could a generation ago," says Paul Wasserman, professor emeritus of librarianship at the University of Maryland (and the subject of an interview in this book). Moreover, he believes, "People are getting frustrated and saying, 'There's so much coming at me. I'll just turn everything off and fly by the seat of my pants.'"

In the past 15 years the world of information has given us a personal computer on every desk. It is often linked to an internal network (Intranet) or an external network (Internet) that can access and transfer a myriad of forms of information that includes information from commercial online databases, CD-ROM, and multimedia. Over this period, much attention and money in business environments has been given to the technology: the conduits of electronic and digital data and information. Yet only limited resources have been spent on the retrieval and use of information or the content of the information accessed. And the least attention has been paid to help knowledge workers understand and acquire the skills to find and work with information content and to integrate these skills into the work environment. In fact, it appears that knowledge workers in this post-industrial society are stuck somewhere between data and information, with a long way to go before they achieve full understanding and knowledge, and only a slight chance of attaining wisdom anytime in the near future.

As businesses and organizations move farther into the Information Age, more and more books will reach the bookstores about how to work and live in it. Scott Adams's popular "Dilbert" comic strips put a hilarious spin on how management is coping with issues of business process reengineering and information technology in the settings of Total Quality

Management (TQM), Benchmarking, ISO 9000, downsizing, and other management practices. In his introduction to *The Dilbert Principle: A Cubicle's Eye View of Bosses, Meetings, Management Fads & Other Workplace Afflictions*,[3] Adams states: "No matter how absurd I try to make the comic strip, I can't stay ahead of what people are experiencing in their own workplaces."

The absurdities point to the need to develop a deeper appreciation and understanding of emerging information issues that have affected and will affect all levels and areas of management, knowledge workers, and information consumers in all business environments, large and small. Here are a few issues:

- Concepts people have in their heads about using information are either outmoded or devalued;
- Creative ideas of individuals and the collective knowledge of an organization are not recognized or organized so that they can be retrieved or used;
- There are, more often than not, no information policies, strategies, or standards that make high-quality internal or external information readily available or people accountable or willing to budget for it;
- If information is available, it is likely that there is no one within the organization who has the authority to ask the right questions;
- If one has the authority, many times one does not know how to ask the right questions to retrieve the information;
- In many cases, someone else in the company or organization already has the information, but is not motivated to share it;
- If information is retrieved, there is rarely someone who knows how to analyze it—or wants to;
- If the information is somehow retrieved and analyzed, it may never be acted upon;
- If acted upon, it may already be outdated, incomplete, or inaccurate;
- If outdated, incomplete, or inaccurate, it can cause a company, organization, or individual to fail in any given situation.

With continued ignorance of and lack of attention to these important Information Age issues, it may be that Drucker's "knowledge workers" will end up as did Greek mythology's Sisyphus, who was doomed by the gods to the labor and frustration of pushing a boulder to the top of a mountain, only to have it roll back on him...for an eternity. In other words, the explosion of information resources is threatening to manage *us*. And most importantly, there can be no knowledge management without an intelligent understanding of the value of information and the complex set of competencies required to retrieve and use it.

Figure I.1 The Sisyphus Dilemma

Notes

1.   Peter Drucker, *Post-Capitalist Society* (New York: HarperCollins Publishers, 1993), 6.

2.   Ibid, 8.

3. Scott Adams, *The Dilbert Principle: A Cubicle's Eye View of Bosses, Meetings, Management Fads & Other Workplace Afflictions* (New York: Harper Business, 1996), or go to Dilbert's homepage at http://www.unitedmedia.com/comics/dilbert/.

For More Information

There is a wealth of practical and theoretical knowledge about print and electronic information retrieval and usage issues, i.e., infothink, available in the literature of the information sciences, business, professional associations, and now on the Internet. Here are some places to begin:

- American Society for Information Science (ASIS)—a society founded in 1937 for information professionals who focus on ways to improve access to information. Go to http://www.asis. org.
- American Library Association (ALA)—the largest association representing school, public, academic, and special libraries. Go to http://www.ala.org.
- Special Libraries Association (SLA)—an international professional organization with 14,000 members in corporate, academic, government, museum, and nonprofit organizations. Go to http://www.sla.org.
- Association of College and Research Libraries (ACRL), a division of ALA—includes over 11,000 academic and research librarians whose mission is to facilitate learning, research, and the scholarly communication process. Go to http://www.ala. org/acrl.htm.
- American Association of School Librarians (AASL)—a division of ALA, provides support for the development of school library media programs and school library media professionals. Go to http://www.ala.org/aasl.
- Library Instruction Roundtable (LIRT)—a roundtable of ALA, features information and news on library instruction to school, public, and academic libraries. Go to http://nervm.nerdc.ufl. edu/~hsswww/lirt/lirt.html.

- The Association for Library and Information Science Education (ALISE)—devoted to the advancement of knowledge and learning in the interdisciplinary field of information studies. Go to http://www.alise.org.
- CRISTAL-ED—Curriculum planning, prototyping courses for the core curriculum and specializations, educational approaches, task force reports. A collaborative project of the School of Information at the University of Michigan with the support of the W. K. Kellogg Foundation. Go to http://www.si.umich.edu/cristaled/.
- Online, Inc.—publisher of *Online*, *Database*, and *Media Professional* publications. Go to the homepage at http://www.onlineinc.com.
- *Information Today*—a newspaper for users and producers of electronic services. Go to http://www.infotoday.com/it/itnew.htm.
- *Link-Up, The Newsmagazine for Users of Online Services*, CD-ROM, and the Internet, at http://www.infotoday.com.
- *The Searcher: The Magazine for Database Professionals*—produced by Barbara Quint, online expert, at http://www.infotoday.com/searcher.
- *Current Cites*—an annotated monthly bibliography of selected articles, books, or electronic documents on information technology. Go to http://www.sunsite.berkeley.edu/CurrentCites/1997.
- For an important historical perspective on electronic information after the first ten years of its introduction, with then current predictions of the future, read the 10th Anniversary Issue of *Database* (October 1988).
- For a historical perspective on the emergence and development of electronic information, see "20 Years of Memories, Reflections, and Prophecies of the Evolution of the Online/Electronic World" in the 20th Anniversary Issue of *Online* (January/February 1997).
- Microsoft Library on the Internet—a benchmark for corporate library sites created by Microsoft's professional librarians for Microsoft employees. Go to http://www.library.microsoft.com.

Part 1   Executive Users of Information

Profiles

Executive users of information in business environments are, in general usage, referred to as "end users" or "information consumers." They are considered the ultimate users of information, whether gathered by themselves or by an information provider or intermediary. Information is used as a tool to provide support or to enhance specialized decision-making requirements. They are generally "in the trenches," the professionals, the knowledge workers, the managers, the decision-makers, and/or they have a direct link to decision makers. End users can have such diverse titles as CEO, CIO, senior manager, administrative assistant, corporate secretary, or even college intern or data entry specialist, and new titles and positions for users of information in business are rapidly developing as more people use information in the workplace. Information seeking and usage on the Internet, commercial online databases, or a print library collection are usually secondary to their jobs. And as you would expect, there is no formal training for library or information usage. Many use consumer-oriented databases, such as CompuServe and America Online, for research and as a gateway to the Internet.

Executive users often have access to data or information created within the company. Their job is to apply information that has been gathered or to see that someone in upper management gets it, and they may require or seek an intermediary to help locate it. Although budget, policy, and privacy issues may determine the use of an intermediary, executive users increasingly require someone within or outside the organization to provide for their specialized information needs. Executive users represented in this book include the following:

Paul Houston, President, Results Management Consultants, Denver, Colorado

Paul Houston, business information expert and management consultant to CEOs, says a corporate strategic plan without focused information is like "firing when blind and crippled." Houston's military education, his experience as a naval intelligence officer in the Far East, and his years as a business executive now enable him to gather business intelligence about a company's opportunities and competition, to analyze the meaning of the information, and then to translate the information to improve corporate strategy.

Alan M. Rifkin, Managing Partner; Rifkin, Livingston & Silver, LLC; Attorneys at Law; Annapolis, Maryland

An attorney for legislative advocacy, Alan Rifkin describes how he and his staff gather and analyze a broad variety of information related to the 90-day state legislative process, why information is the critical basis for decision making, and how it can have long-lasting positive or negative implications.

Steven L. Lubetkin, Director; Global Ratings Development, Standard & Poor's Rating Services; New York, New York

A corporate (de facto) information gatekeeper, Steven Lubetkin explains that one of his roles at Standard & Poor's Global Ratings Services is to identify and communicate critical information to help bond and credit analysts analyze and present complex financial and credit methodologies to their corporate clients, including financial intermediaries, investment bankers, brokers, portfolio managers, institutional investors, analysts, and executives.

Samuel B. Hopkins, President, Hopkins & Associates, Baltimore, Maryland

Information technology consultant Sam Hopkins provides analysis and implementation of computer technology to law firms. He describes the many information resources he must use to keep up with the ever-changing world of computer technology and software for his clients.

Barbara E. Doty, President, Majority Asset Management, Inc., Baltimore, Maryland
Investment advisor to individual and corporate clients, Barbara Doty believes that "successful investments and acceptable ideas to investors are a function of what people are hearing or appear to believe." She provides insight into the world of investment information and shares techniques and resources she uses to determine people's perceptions.

Susan J. Ganz, President, Lion Brothers, Inc., Baltimore, Maryland
As CEO of a major emblem manufacturing company, Susan Ganz discusses the importance of ideas gained through reading and personal contacts and the difficulties of translating information from the nebulous world of concepts into the concrete world of specific products for her company.

Phyllis Brotman, President, Image Dynamics, Inc., Baltimore, Maryland
Public relations executive Phyllis Brotman explains how her childhood experiences prepared her for a public relations career and formed her knowledge base for working in media. She also provides examples of programs she has created and the information resources used to create them.

For More Information

Although there are academic studies that have followed the usage and needs of information end users in science and technology—e.g., engineers, scientists, R&D departments—there have been few studies that specifically focus on the requirements of end users in business environments who are accessing or learning to access information, particularly of the electronic type. There are, however, a few worth noting:
* For an in-depth analysis of changing information user categories, read the article, "The Information Consumer in Transition," by

online spokesperson Barbara Quint in *Changing Roles in Information Distribution*, Ann Marie Cunningham and Wendy Wicks, eds. (Philadelphia: National Federation of Abstracting and Information Services, 1993), 113-136.

- In 1994, approximately 85 percent of organizations report having some end users accessing online databases, according to a survey of 88 organizations as reported by Jean Fisher and Susanne Bjorner, "Enabling Online End-User Searching," *Special Libraries* 85, 4 (Fall 1994): 281-291.

In discussing issues related to managing online access and training of end users, Bjorner reports her own experiences in training end users to use online services at IBM's training sessions: "Students reported that they couldn't be away from their primary work tasks for a full day for this activity. Rather, they needed more time to check their voice mail for emergency messages from managers and coworkers, and they couldn't sit and concentrate for such a long time."

The results of the 1994 study are still relevant in the workplace, but the remarkable growth and development of the Internet since then has changed the workplace environment significantly, as well as the way in which users and uses of electronic and digital information are being categorized.

- See "Environmental Scanning by CEOs in Two Canadian Industries," in the *Journal of the American Society for Information Science* 44:4 (May 1993): 194-203. This study by Ethel Auster and Chun Wei Choo presents findings from interviews with 250 CEOs of telecommunication and publishing firms, how they acquire and use information about the internal and external business environment, and what value is placed on it.
- Chun Wei Choo, *Information Management for the Intelligent Organization, The Art of Scanning the Environment*, ASIS Monograph Series (Medford, NJ: Information Today, 1995). See "Summary of Research on Managers as Information Users" on page 56.

Chapter 1   A Business Intelligence Expert

Paul Houston

What enables the wise sovereign and the good general to strike and conquer, and achieve things beyond the reach of ordinary men, is foreknowledge.

Sun Tzu,
On the Art of War (500 B.C.),
Translated by R. L. Wing, 1988

"Competitive Intelligence (CI) is not industrial espionage; it is business intelligence. In fact, in recognized competitive intelligence circles, it is the legal and ethical gathering of information, 95 percent of which is readily available from public sources. One of the most important elements of CI is the gathering of information on your competitors and competitive situations. It is important to monitor companies that are actively competing with us, now and in the future, because they can affect our profitability and ultimately our survival," says Paul Houston.

Houston likes to tell the story of how he's been in the intelligence field since the tender age of eleven:

> I was in a very competitive little league and my grandfather, who was very analytical, suggested that I ought to be down at the ballpark with a clipboard observing the other team's strategies so that I could learn how to pitch to the opponents. I remember sitting there and observing these guys and seeing what their signals were and watching how they played and how they shifted different batters and their strategies for base running. And I remember playing them and

beating them! It was like "this is the way to go in life!" It was a real
lesson.

Paul Houston graduated from the U.S. Naval Academy at the height
of the Cold War with a degree in modern European history and a minor
in the Russian language. This training and education enticed him further
into intelligence work and the analysis that went with it. After graduation
from the Naval Academy, Houston then spent five more years as a naval
intelligence officer stationed around the Indian Ocean and the Far East.
"Our constant focus was monitoring the world situation and analyzing the
strategic and tactical moves of the Soviet navy within that context."

From Naval Intelligence to
Business Intelligence

Houston explains that in the standard course on naval intelligence,
he learned to plan "alpha strikes" and to brief aircrews on specific targets.
"You certainly learn oppositional and tactical thinking when you are
trying to figure out what an enemy submarine is up to and how they are
deploying their forces," he says.

After the navy, Houston got an MBA in finance. He then joined a
start-up company in the field of business information that produced and
marketed audiotapes of best business articles from over 100 weekly
publications. He was president of the company until it was sold in 1991,
and he then was an investigative journalist in the oil industry, mainly
related to the former Soviet Union. This allowed him to maintain his
language ability by writing pieces about the many changes that were
taking place in Russia.

Results Management Consultants

On January 1, 1993, Houston became a full-time management
consultant and founded Results Management Consultants in Denver,
Colorado. In his words, he helps companies "improve their competitive-
ness and thus become more profitable quicker." He does that through
"investigation, analysis, planning, and accountability," which involve
looking at a company's internal strengths and weaknesses while also

evaluating opportunities and threats from the outside. He also helps his clients figure out answers to such questions as Where are we now? Where do we want to get to? How are we going to get there? And how will we know when we have arrived?

The Reverse Competitive Analysis Technique and Learning the Terrain

Houston's earlier experiences in naval intelligence and business management led him toward business intelligence, a process linked to the competitive intelligence process. He explains that the CI process is intertwined with both an internal and an external look at a company. In fact, he says that you can't separate the two. He describes how some forward-thinking companies use the "reverse competitive analysis technique" to understand internal issues. "They hire a consultant to take a hard look at their company from an external viewpoint by watching and talking to customers and suppliers and selected industry sources to discover how the company is perceived in terms of strengths and weaknesses. Not too many CEOs have the ego strength to do that. But for those who do, it is extremely valuable," says Houston.

Another way of taking a look at internal strengths and weaknesses is through "diagnostic interviewing," i.e., studying operational and financial data, looking at organizational issues, interviewing, and looking at results. "That's obviously where CI has a strong role, and there it's a matter of looking at the whole wide world around the company," says Houston.

Ready, Fire, Aim

Houston explains that one of the mistakes companies typically make, even when they accept that competitive intelligence is important, is to come up with a "rifle shot project." He says that once the company gets what executives think is the answer, they use it to solve the immediate problem and then go on to another crisis.

A well-designed system of competitive intelligence is an ongoing information gathering process that's in sync with the plans of the company. Hiring outside consultants can create problems, because consultants sometimes come in and find the problem, fix it, then leave. But on the other hand, a consultant who understands this kind of issue can also suggest that it might be very beneficial to set up a more formal ongoing CI process by building an internal staff.

Developing a System and Procedures

Houston emphasizes that the most important element for the success of any company is that there needs to be an internal champion of the CI process:

> Ideally that would be the CEO or a senior executive. It takes top management's interest, which too often we don't have. If we can get top management to see the need, they give it the blessing and say to their staff: "This fellow is going to be talking to you in the next couple of days, so please share what you know with him, because he has my full confidence, and what he is doing is very important for our company's survival and for your job." That usually gets their attention.
>
> Companies don't always need to set up a separate functional CI area, but they need to build awareness throughout the company about what is valuable and what isn't. Quite often, the VP-marketing will assume the CI function within his or her job description.
>
> A company needs to set up a procedure for reporting. For example, if someone is at a trade show and hears something that is a potential danger signal for the company, there should be a procedure in place where the person can report back the data so it can be analyzed and related to something else that management might already know.

Houston says that "many of the important signals are detected at such a low level of the company that they never quite get to the top in time. That's why it's very important to develop a procedure, because whether you have a dedicated CI function or not, you could still have an effective system with procedures."

The CI Audit and Needs Assessment:
Reading the Tea Leaves

Houston describes several of the most successful procedures he uses to develop CI within a client company:

> The first step in the CI process would be to interview management, review their plans, visions, and goals, and analyze what types of things might be happening both inside and outside the company that are significant.
>
> Next, identify the key intelligence issues and develop an understanding of where those issues are played out. At that point, one could go to key reports of top management and develop a user interest profile or needs assessment. For example, if executives will be users of intelligence, what do they need to know? What types of intelligence information would help them make better decisions and do their job better?
>
> Finally, determine what intelligence resources already exist within the company in terms of files, memos, special reports, industry contacts, etc. Debriefing key executives and employees concerning their knowledge of competitors and the external environment is critical. This process of identifying, locating, and cataloging internal knowledge and assets is called the "CI Audit."

Houston continues his discussion:

> If you perform good diagnostic interviews and develop accurate user interest profiles, you can usually see about three or four areas where the company should be doing a better job of pulling in information, collecting information in one place, "reading the tea leaves," and making decisions based on it. I think that's critical to point out, because historically, governments and businesses have usually had the information they needed somewhere around them, they just haven't identified, analyzed, and disseminated it properly.

Staring a Marvelous Piece of
Intelligence Analysis in the Face

Houston says there is a well-defined difference between information gathering (which is the collection) and transforming that information into intelligence (which is the analysis) and then the acting on it intelligently (which is dissemination and decision making). Those are the three steps and there is a breakdown at each level:

> There are basic skills and ways of thinking that some people lack, so they aren't as good collectors as they could be. Then, there are people who avoid the hard labor of thinking, so they don't do good analysis, and then, even those who pass the first two hurdles often are staring a marvelous piece of intelligence analysis in the face, and they don't recognize it and act on it. If you miss any one of the three, you are out. You don't necessarily have to be good at all three. You might only be good at one, but you need to bring a complementary team around you that, as a team, is good at collection, analysis, and dissemination. Many times, CI people think they have done a complete collection effort, but there are several key elements missing. Therefore, even if they do use the right thinking skills, they will end up with a faulty conclusion.

For his clients, Houston writes a summary analysis, because it is important to focus the company's thoughts. He summarizes by identifying key areas where there is opportunity for improving and identifying company strengths. He then makes recommendations for action. "If you can raise the awareness in certain key areas, clients can see the rewards very quickly," says Houston.

The "Blindspot"

Although there are a number of competitive intelligence books on the market, Houston refers to Benjamin Gilad's *Business Blindspots,*[1] which says that there is a "blindspot" issue for CEOs, where they are blinded to contrary evidence in many cases. Houston explains that they might say: "We launched that major project, and it was a brilliant move. The expert over there who pointed out that it may not be such a good idea or that it needs to be modified must be insane."

"The blindspot issue is an important psychological hurdle to overcome," says Houston. He cites the 1996 assassination of Israeli Prime Minister Itzhak Rabin:

> The highly sophisticated Israeli intelligence services had hard evidence regarding a potential assassination, but the process failed

because the lead was given in a very roundabout way. Police said they were "blinded" to the possibility that a threat to the Prime Minister's life could come from an Israeli citizen and so rejected contrary evidence. This lesson applies directly to business intelligence situations.

The Hard Labor of Thinking

The blindspot issues can also be the result of faulty thinking skills. Houston believes good thinking skills are not utilized enough in government, business, or politics. He quotes Harvey Firestone, the great tire executive: "There is no extent to which a man will not go to avoid the hard labor of thinking." If more CEOs remembered that, Houston says that there would be more prosperous companies with a bias for activity (maybe not action, but activity). "Yeah, let's get that report done. Let's get to that meeting," the CEOs say.

Houston asks: "How about if we sat back, took a hard look at our plans and our competitors and our resources and our core competencies, and decided what we should really be doing? That's hard work!"

Identifying Key Intelligence Issues—An Anecdote About an Information Problem

Houston gives an example of how he helped a client company identify its key intelligence issues: He saw an opportunity to help this client, a large international oil company involved in a Central Asian venture. The company was being blindsided by constant change in its external environment. Houston went to the head of public affairs and to several key executives and suggested that the principal problem was that there was a serious information gap. He suggested they needed to develop much more insight regarding the politics and personalities of the Central Asian region where they were having problems. He showed them how a simple, inexpensive, low-tech process of monitoring several dozen newspapers in the former Soviet Union on a regular basis would answer a lot of their questions and provide them with an opportunity to be proactive.

While Houston was in Moscow on another assignment, he collected over 70 different Russian newspapers and magazines, scanned them, and found about 20 different articles that related to the region and types of concerns the company had. He had them translated for the company and presented the executives with one particular article about the president of the newly independent country who was coming to visit the company the very next week. "There was a huge interview with the president in the publication about all his aspirations, his attitude toward foreign investments, his lifetime goals, and his goals for his country, all of the things that this oil company could have an influence on," says Houston.

The outcome?

> They loved it at the time, but it wasn't in anyone's job description to maintain that function. I have kept up with them since then, and they didn't maintain that simple process [company name withheld for confidentiality], and as you might have read, they've cut their funding by 90 percent, and they have lost several hundred million dollars of the shareholders' money largely because they didn't understand the overall environment they were operating in. This is a pretty pronounced story, but it's a dramatic one, and it shows how they really could have made a difference if they had had a better intelligence function. A subsequent *Wall Street Journal* article said that the loss of significant revenue signaled a significantly gloomier outlook for what they described as the crown jewel of their overseas growth strategy.

The American Cultural Bias Against Intelligence

What Houston had done was offer his client a steady stream of intelligence:

> They were all open sources, none of it clandestine stuff. But for whatever reason, Americans tend to have a bias against intelligence which French, Japanese, or Russian executives certainly don't have. Typically, foreign international executives tend to value intelligence more than American executives. They tend to see the value of it right away. We have a culture where we think, "That's spying." In actuality, most foreign executives would admire an American company if they found out they actually scanned public sources on a consistent

basis. If the foreign executive ever approached them about it, the American company could say, "We realize we are visitors in your country, and we realize we have a lot to learn, and we are a learning organization. We want to be a good corporate citizen of your country, and we would never want to offend someone or do something less than optimum for your people. Therefore, we have a vested interest in being extremely smart and sensitive to your issues." It could be turned into a great positive.

Learning Japanese Methods of Gathering Information and Intelligence

Houston cites another example of where he has been involved in negotiations with executives, this time the Japanese:

> It is absolutely clear: I don't think any Japanese executives ever went into a meeting with an American executive where they hadn't prepared thoroughly and in advance with personal intelligence profiles on the American executive, including their interests, their hobbies, their family situations, where they were born, raised, educated, what type of career they have had, what their key decisions were in their career, where they were considered especially competent. And yet, American executives tend to go into the negotiation with at best a cursory little review of where their Japanese counterpart was from and the company they generally represent, and they think they can go in with a warm handshake, a quick wit, and a sharp brain. They generally get skinned alive.

How would the Japanese be able to get that information? Houston explains how they set up good networks in the United States, "and the Japanese don't hesitate to utilize research companies on their behalf, but very few American executives would even think about it!"

Bias Toward Action, Not Reflection

Houston provides insight into his experience in working with executives:

American executives are extremely action-oriented. It is hard to get
their attention. Most senior level executives are even more action-
oriented, with less attention on reflective skills. The good ones do
more thinking and reflecting. They should think like people of action
and act like people of thought. The corporate culture is often, "Don't
rock the boat," and a good intelligence officer rocks the boat.

Essential Elements of Information

The Essential Elements of Information (EEIs) are one of the key
analytical techniques used in the CI process. Houston describes this as a
useful technique for working with a company that is going through the
initial planning process:

> Suppose we develop a vision, we look at the situation around
> us, and we develop a mission statement based on that vision as a
> rallying cry; and then we try to develop objectives. It would be
> helpful to be able to ask: "What types of things might blow us out of
> the water? What might derail our plans?"

Houston continues:

> The EEIs would be the mandate for the ongoing CI monitoring
> and would say such things as: "We need to follow XYZ competitors
> in terms of their market share and their industry. Or we could pick the
> following three companies as a proxy, because if they start hiring
> research chemists with this type of background, it will imply that they
> will be entering our marketplace two years sooner than we
> anticipated."

Houston says that the more specific you can be about what you need
to know, the better off you will be, and that if more time is spent asking
up-front questions, the answer is already halfway provided.

Information Gaps

When you talk about EEIs, Houston says you also need to talk about
information gaps. For instance, he might say to a client that he

recommends starting with a literature search and looking at everything that can be gained through open sources. And then he would say:

> Okay, what are the gaps here? What don't we know? We don't have any idea of what the local newspaper has been saying about them. We need to close that gap. And then it's a matter of what would be the most cost-effective means of closing that gap. It may be an ongoing database monitoring program, talking to sources, developing sources in a different field than we have now. It may be activating sources that we already know about and just haven't used in a while, or it may be bringing together what information we already have inside our own company. That's often the case. A lot of this information resides in the company in "functional silos," and nobody even knows it. That's one of the reasons for going around the company and doing awareness briefings and some diagnostic interviewing. Some of the questions you ask are: "Where do you find sources? What sources do you have here? Who do you talk to on a regular basis? What kind of periodicals do you get? What trade shows do you go to on a regular basis?"

Houston says that the person who would conduct the awareness briefings and diagnostic interviewing often is the market research/competitive intelligence person under the VP of marketing, or the corporate librarian. "It is a matter of who is the best interviewer," he claims.

Tactical Information Versus Strategic Information

Houston thinks CEOs in general do a pretty good job of collecting and using tactical information, but in terms of strategic information, they are pretty weak. For example, he says that a strategy within the corporate environment might be to slowly become the premium-priced competitor over time. A tactic to accomplish this would be to cut prices over the short term. The strategic plan is future oriented and long term while the tactic is short term or immediate.

Houston continues:

> In general, the only way to really gather strategic information on an ongoing basis is to set up a CI process within the company and

have some type of a working, functional CI procedure and a monitoring process and to have either outside advisors or an internal intelligence person who really is independent and isn't worried about his/her next promotion. That's a key issue, because we have a lot of yes people and pleasers and job holders who really have to couch their recommendations in "bureaucratese." What CEOs need is an independent person who can say, "I know that's your strategy, but here's what the market seems to be saying. It seems to be saying that your multimillion dollar proposed investment in X may not work out, or maybe you need to be working with some different officials, or whatever, because the ones you are working with now don't seem to have the ear of the big guy." It's very hard for a job holder to say those types of things to a CEO, who generally doesn't like to hear bad news.

Setting Up a "Kitchen Cabinet"

Typically, there is no management slot for that kind of position. Houston says that it would have to be an outside manager, or a board member who comes in and isn't really desperate for the monthly fee. "It has to be someone who can literally tell the CEO, 'you are wrong!'" Once again, Houston cites Gilad, who recommends that the position should be filled by someone the president sets up in the office of the president as part of the "kitchen cabinet" but not filled by someone on the strategic planning staff. "It should be someone who has a place at the table but doesn't get involved in all the games and political posturing and whatever else that goes on in most large corporations," says Houston.

"This person is hard to find," he acknowledges. "Gilad calls it the Director of Competitive Learning, and has defined it is his book this way":

> Now, take the two separate organizational innovations, the china-breaker perspective of organizational change and the concept of a powerful office of the president, and put them together with the new competitive intelligence process to create this synergy: The director of competitive learning, the decoder of early signals whose chief assignment is to gather information that will enable management to fight the onset of blindspots, must be the top level's china breaker and must be located in a reorganized office of the president.[2]

A Houston Recommendation for Success: The Competitive Advantage of Politicians

Houston offers a suggestion on how to develop a competitive advantage:

> I am thinking about CEOs. And this you will probably not hear from anyone else: A CEO could learn a lot from a politician. A good politician thinks about CI far, far deeper and broader than almost any CEO I have ever met. CEOs don't think about competitive reaction enough. They say, "Oh, we will cut prices, and they may or may not respond, but that's a good move for us." But a real learning experience would be to get involved in a political race where a fairly savvy politician is up against an entrenched incumbent. That would be a tremendous CI learning experience for a CEO. It would be on-the-job learning and watching a way of thinking as the campaign committee proceeds through and then gets information on the incumbent. This is generally called "opposition research." And the key would be to learn how they used the information against that incumbent.

Where Houston Is Now

As an extension of his management consultancy, Houston has recently added competitive intelligence placement and hiring services. Over the last few years, he has become interested in the people side of CI and has found that companies do less than optimum job searching for CI professionals, because "no one understands what they do. It's mushy," says Houston, "like hiring a vice president of creative [development]."

Now, Houston provides his CI expertise to help companies define what kind of CI professional would fit within a particular company culture. He locates, screens, interviews, and investigates potential winning candidates for companies who are hiring CI professionals. He says that sometimes executives who are hiring might say something like, "We want a cowboy here," or "We want somebody who fits in well and can say something politically smooth and build respect."

"*That* is a challenge," Houston says, "especially since CI is growing so fast, and there is such a shortage of good talent for all that is required."

But with Paul Houston's well-honed personal and CI instincts, if the talent is there, he will find it.

Notes

1.   Benjamin Gilad, *Business Blindspots, Replacing Your Company's Entrenched and Outdated Myths, Beliefs and Assumptions with the Realities of Today's Markets* (Chicago: Probus Publishing Company, 1995).
2.   *Business Blindspots*, 198.

For More Information

I.   Information resources for management and competitor intelligence:

- The Institute of Management Consultants homepage—http://www.imcusa.org
- Society of Competitor Intelligence Professionals (SCIP) homepage—http://www.scip.org
- Society of Competitor Intelligence Professionals (SCIP) Curriculum Modules for Educational Programs that include competencies for intelligence professionals, CI curriculum guidelines, and the competitive intelligence cycle provided by Jerry P. Miller of Simmons College—http:/www.scip/org/miller.html
- The Gilad-Herring Academy of Competitive Intelligence, 703-549-9500
- R.L. Wing, *The Art of Strategy, A New Translation of SunTzu's Classic, The Art of War*, Main Street Books (New York: Doubleday, 1988)
- D.A. Benton, *How to Think Like a CEO* (New York: Warner Books, 1996)
- Mark McNeilly, *Sun Tzu and the Art of Business* homepage—http://casmedia.com/suntzu

II.   The continuation of a Q&A session describing what Houston uses to stay informed:

MP: What sources of information do you use for your work?

PH: I use a wide range of information and publications. I subscribe to the *Wall Street Journal, Direct Marketing News (DM News), Sales and Marketing Management, Marketing Tools, Direct Marketing Magazine, Competitive Intelligence Review, Institute of Management Consultants Journal, Inc.,* and two local Denver newspapers every day and Sunday. I scan the *New York Times* in the library, as well as *Forbes, Fortune, Business Week* and *Vital Speeches of the Day.* Just a cursory glance at *Vital Speeches* every two weeks, and I will often see a speech by someone in a related field or someone in a client's field or in my own field.

I also look at the Reuter's feed daily from CompuServe and I watch the MacNeil Lehrer News Hour. I believe I am doing far more than most CEOs, who would not have the time to do all of that on a daily basis, but since I am an information consultant, in many ways, it's part of my work.

I scan the trade press for every client I have. So I've recently added periodicals on direct broadcast satellite and cable. I have to have a lot of discipline. I don't pile things up. I go through my publications, rip and file, and read when I need. I do not allow piles to grow, because, as you can imagine, it would get out of control very quickly. When you follow information on a day-in-day-out basis consistently, your mind detects subtle changes.

MP: Of all of these resources you are using, which would you consider the most important?

PH: What everybody has to look at daily is the *Wall Street Journal.* That's the newspaper of record for the world of business, which is the world I operate in except for the world of politics. But that's another story. Actually, even for politics. The *Wall Street Journal* is such a critical source.

MP: What would you read for your international coverage?

PH: I get that from what I just described. But there's also *The Economist* of London, and the *Financial Times* of London. But if I had to go to Japan (of course, I don't follow it on a daily basis), I would read back issues of the *Asian Wall Street Journal, Asia Week,* and *Nikkei Business* (a periodical). These are all critical, and anyone who does business on a regular basis with Japan should be looking at all three.

In Russia, there is a plethora of Russian language sources available, and I do read them from time to time. For example, *Moscow News* is an extremely good one, and *Kommersant* is the best one. And anyone who is doing business in Russia could subscribe to them. Both come out in translation form as well. There are some publications in Russia that aren't translated but that are just absolutely fascinating reads, like *Independent* newspaper. If one is trying to get sophisticated coverage of the politics in Moscow and certain business issues, one could read that, too.

We could take almost any country. For instance, I am helping a client who is trying to do a lot of business in Mexico, and we are setting up a CI process. On my next visit down there, I will be bringing a satchel of periodicals I found just on Mexico. They are springing up like mushrooms (in the U.S., especially around the manufacturing belt around the border). They are very helpful, and they identify the key issues, trends, developments, and the key people to contact.

I also like to listen to shortwave broadcasts in countries where my clients do business. One of my favorites is the BBC Monitoring Service, which provides programs on the business climate, the economy, and profiles of local business or political figures. They provide transcripts or a written digest of broadcasts. The other is *FBIS, the Foreign Broadcasting Information Service and Monitoring Times* (703-837-9200), which provides times and frequencies of broadcasts.

MP: Do you use CompuServe or America Online or any of the consumer-oriented databases?

PH: I'm a pretty low-tech guy. If I do a sophisticated database search, I hire an information broker, because I think it is something they spend a lot of time on, and they know all the nuances. I would say "here are the search parameters." But for my own stuff, looking at *Reuters* on *CompuServe* is enough. I spend a lot of time on low-tech thinking skills, which means I use the most sophisticated computer ever created, the brain. Beyond that, it's pretty standard. I use the PC, telephone, voice mail, fax, e-mail, and audiocassettes, so I can listen to business ideas while I drive.

MP: Do you have any favorite things you like to read for pleasure?

PH: I do so much in business that it is important to look at some other things for enjoyment. I enjoy reading certain alternative newspapers that do investigative reporting as opposed to the mainline press that tends to get coopted by the powers that be, and won't cover the tough stories and won't dig in and find out what's happening in the City Council, for instance. I find that sharpens my mind. There's a wonderful newspaper in the Rocky Mountain area called *Westword*. Their articles really attack some sacred cows and do some good investigative writing. Let's face it, the investigative journalists are close cousins to CI practitioners.

I enjoy political reading, such as the *New Republic* and the *National Review*. I read the *American Spectator*, because they do some investigative journalism, which I enjoy, and I read some things you would find unusual. I glance through *Mad Magazine* for a laugh as well as something I just discovered called *Funny Times*, which is where I find business cartoons that I use with clients. And I like Elmore Leonard mysteries. And while I don't read a constant diet of this, I like Russian literature, usually in English. I especially enjoy Gogol; reading a Gogol novel in Russian is quite an undertaking, even if you are fluent.

MP: What did he write and when?

PH: *Dead Souls* is the main one, and he wrote in the late 19th century about rural Russia.

MP: That sounds like it could be pretty serious.

PH: It is a fascinating work, and I found myself dropping the book laughing so hard at his humor. Actually, it's a good book to read if you are doing personal intelligence profiles on people, because Gogol's insight into the human character is quite penetrating.

MP: What about organizations? Which ones do you find useful
       for networking?

PH: The Institute of Management Consultants (212-697-8262)
       is the 30-year-old organization representing mostly indepen-
       dent management consultants. They have a very strong code
       of ethics, i.e., you put the clients' needs ahead of your own,
       no self-dealing, full disclosure, and dedication to advancing
       the state of the art in management consulting. They publish
       The Institute of Management Consultant's Journal.

       The Society of Competitive Intelligence Professionals
       (703-739-0696) is also an important industry trade group
       growing rapidly and representing competitive intelligence
       professionals around the world. (Houston was founding
       chairperson of the Rocky Mountain SCIP chapter.) Their
       publication, *Competitive Intelligence Review*, is well worth
       reading. Their code of ethics is also very important to read
       to clear up misconceptions about the role and value of
       competitive intelligence within the organization.

MP: Who are the intelligence gurus you most admire?

PH: Ben Gilad is the best in my estimation. He likes to shatter
       myths, and he is provocative. I also like Leonard Fuld and
       Kirk Tyson.

III.   How other cultures think about information and intelligence:

Jean-Marie Bonthaus, CI consultant in New York and Paris and
guest lecturer at New York University, wrote a comparative article
about countries with strong CI cultures in "Understanding Intelligence Across Cultures" *International Journal of Intelligence and
Counterintelligence* 6,4 (December 1993). Bonthaus says that
different beliefs about intelligence lead to different attitudes and
practices that in turn create different intelligence abilities and
disabilities. Here are excerpts:

> *On Germany:* Where U.S. intelligence is satisfied with
> bullet points of data, the Germans require complete
> descriptions and give considerable importance to history
> as a determinant of current business...German intelligence
> seeks comprehensive procedural descriptions, especially

of competitors, management and planning processes... They like procedures to be precisely spelled out and to remain constant, resulting in a lack of flexibility in their organizations' responses to intelligence signals.

On France: French executives often have a glass office in the center of an open floor so as to remain in the flow of information...the French model is authoritarian and autocratic...French companies do not maintain codes of ethics, perceiving them as an irrelevant Anglo-Saxon concept...while the French seek sophistication in the formulation of questions, the Americans look for simplicity in answers.

On Sweden: All Swedish victories have been achieved through extraordinary intelligence, brilliant political diplomacy, and economic maneuvering. In addition to its prominent business intelligence network, the Swedish system is organized into civilian, economic, and psychological defense sectors, to help people resist a potential aggressor...Sweden has developed and teaches a humanistic, holistic approach to intelligence...Intelligence is part of an overall system to monitor internal and external stability, educate officials, citizens, and foreign partners regarding emerging conditions, organizations, and personalities.

On Japan: The pledge of allegiance of the Imperial Kingdom, dating back to 1868, stated that it was every subject's duty to gather information about the rest of the world. The system has been in place for 125 years. It is mature, effective, and efficient...There is only one Japanese word for information and intelligence: JOHO... There are supposedly 380 intelligence companies in Tokyo alone...Intelligence is viewed as a totality: every piece of information is potentially intelligence...Sharing information is encouraged from early childhood.

On the United States: American intelligence is reluctant to look for the best practices outside its own geographical and cultural boundaries...American intelligence prefers to respond to crises rather than to plan...American intelligence has too often served political and corporate policymakers who focused on personal maneuvering

rather than on long-term communitarian strategic planning...Statistics and facts are dearer to American inductive
minds than the concepts and ideas where the French or
Japanese intelligence find meaning...the American
analytical models fail to grasp most interpersonal
messages...This mistrust of nonverbal perception allows
for only limited sets of criteria when scanning other
cultures...

Chapter 2 An Attorney for Legislative Advocacy

Alan M. Rifkin

Advocate, a person called in to plead the cause of another; especially one entitled, as having the right of audience, to plead the cause of another in a court of law.

Encyclopedia Britannica

"In many respects, legislative advocacy is reduced in the public perception to a slap on the back and a hot meal. It is far from that," says Alan Rifkin. He explains that "the most effective legislative advocates are students of the law who understand what the law means, recognize the public policy implications, have done extensive research on the laws in other states, have a good sound legal basis for their positions, and advocate them in the same way that a trial attorney advocates on behalf of his or her client. Advocacy is not a personality process as much as it is an information-driven process and that is where the public perception differs from reality."

The Firm

Rifkin, Livingston, Levitan & Silver, LLC, Attorneys at Law, provide a full range of traditional legal services, including lobbying for clients who are predominantly Fortune 500 companies and institutions. The firm has developed a special niche in state (Maryland) business and political communities, where it carries a lot of clout, and has now become one of the most powerful firms of its kind in the state.

Alan M. Rifkin, managing partner of the firm, draws from his earlier experience as chief legislative officer to the governor of Maryland and counsel to the Senate of Maryland. While in these roles, Rifkin developed and honed his legal, legislative, and political skills. In a state with some 900 lobbyists, Rifkin is now considered one of the most effective available.

Legislative Advocacy and Lobbying

It is clearly important to Rifkin that the legislative process be understood, and he points out:

> The reason lobbying is often misunderstood is because many people don't have a full understanding of the complexities of government and politics. Often it's easier to simplify difficult concepts and to reduce them to the lowest common denominator. However, lobbying is very much a skilled profession and one that is much more open for public display today than ever before. We are highly regulated. We file reports on a biannual basis, we have to register all of our clients, and we have to disclose expenses. These reports get sent to the State Ethics Committee for public review.

Roots in the Magna Carta

Rifkin explains the original role of lobbying in the democratic process:

The history of lobbying goes back to the days of Anglo-Saxon governments and the Magna Carta in 1215. That was the first recognition that any individual could petition the king for redress of grievances. Prior to that time, there was the belief in the sovereignty of kings, and it was not only wrong, in many respects, it was unheard of to challenge the will of an individual who ruled by divine right. The right of an individual to have free speech and the right to petition government for redress of grievances allowed for personal interaction and through many evolutions ultimately resulted in the American form of a participatory democracy. And this is the basis on which businesses, individuals, institutions, charities, and civic groups reach out to their government.

What Drives Lobbying

"There are several major reasons for the proliferation of business and other entities that now petition government," Rifkin says. "One is the growth of government. I have some clients who refer to the fact that in decades past, government used to be their 'silent partner' and is now their 'general partner.' The clients look at 30 to 40 percent of their income as a business expense dedicated to the government by way of taxes. Their businesses are regulated by rules that are ever changing and evolving, and they see that government can affect their business today and in the future by changes in business climate, laws, and rules. These businesses are now taking an active role, because they care what happens."

Rifkin explains that another reason for the growth of advocacy at the state level has been the shift of responsibilities from the federal government to the state government and as that has happened, an ever-growing cadre of individuals and businesses see fit to make sure that government understands their business.

Rifkin believes that state lobbying is a growth industry as government expands or contracts. He explains that because of its location, Maryland is unique:

> Maryland is located between the nation's capital and the northeast corridor and is one of the most significant economic markets—the fourth largest commercial market in the country. So you

have an enormous number of businesses, transportation, and distribution centers, and bank centers all in this very high per-capita commercial marketplace.

The 90-Day Window of Opportunity to Gather, Process, and Present Information

Rifkin describes the legislative process of pleading a client's case in a state court of law:

> Within a 90-day period in Maryland, 188 individuals from all walks of life, many of whom may or may not be in business, or may not have ever been involved in the issues brought before them, are being asked to render, as experts, very specific decisions on hundreds of topics ranging from health care to banking to insurance regulations. Their decisions can have long-lasting positive or negative implications. So it is incumbent on businesses and organizations, charitable groups, and others who care about those decisions to participate. The state legislative process has a finite life. In the condensed time period that you see in government and legislative work, it is not only important but ultimately critical to manage information and communications effectively and rapidly. It is of little value if you know and have access to information and that information isn't transmitted to your clients or the policymakers.

The Progress of a Bill

The state legislature expresses its will through motions, orders, messages, bills, and resolutions voted on by members of the General Assembly represented by elected citizens of the state from all areas of interest and expertise. The passage of a bill is a multifaceted process. Figure 2.1 best illustrates the path taken from "First Reading" to the governor for signature.

Figure 2.1 The Progress of a Bill

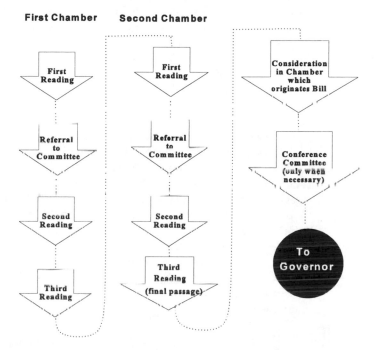

(Excerpted from *Your Voice in Annapolis, Maryland General Assembly*, Annapolis, MD: Department of Fiscal Services, 1995)

The Agenda for the General Assembly

There are hundreds of legislative subjects dealing with such issues as taxes, education, environment, health, welfare, gambling/racing, motorists, and state workers. Here are just a few examples of items taken from a local business newspaper that are considered important to business during the current year's (1997) legislative session:

- *Banking*. Example: Institutional Review—Would change, from one year to 18 months, how often well-managed institutions are reviewed by state agencies, eliminating a requirement that state-chartered institutions publish reports of their financial conditions in area newspapers.

- *Technology*. Example: Technology Transfer—State university researchers want more flexibility in entering into research and development deals with federal labs and industry.
- *Health Care*. Example: Medicaid Reform—As a result of legislation passed last year, the Department of Health and Mental Hygiene will seek a proposal to move most of the state's Medicaid recipients into managed care organizations.
- *Retailing*. Example: Precious Metals—Would amend the state's second hand precious metal law to limit the liability of businesses that turn over stolen jewelry to the police.
- *Real Estate*. Example: Property Tax Payments—To help lower settlement costs; would allow home buyers to pay property taxes in arrears instead of up front when they buy a house.
- *Construction*. Example: Procurement—Would establish definite time frames during which the state must make a response to requests for payment from contractors.
- *Design*. Example: Unlicensed Practitioners—Would increase the power of the state to crack down on unlicensed architects, landscape architects, engineers, surveyors, and certified interior designers.[1]

The Information Process While the Legislature Is in Session: Evolving Moment by Moment

In this fast-paced, short-term environment, Rifkin and his staff of attorneys, legislative assistants, computer assistants, and secretaries are constantly gathering, disseminating, analyzing, and using information to stay informed and to keep clients informed:

> The process of gathering information is the basis of good decision making. This process, whether it is the reading of legislation, the legal analysis, or the technical information, is evolving moment by moment, day by day, as you add new information and the human elements of competing interests, competing pressures, and the other factors that go into the decision-making process for legislators. Gathering information is a process that has no real finite beginning or end. So you almost have to view what you know now as the baseline for what you will learn later in the day.

You need to be able to connect various forms of information and then be able to do what no computer and no information technology system can do...analyze the information. If you are in a scientific setting, the analysis of data can be done on raw material and raw information, and you can come up with a logical answer. What makes government unique is the fact that there is the human element that may or may not track the scientific data and may actually lead to other conclusions. And so, in our business, information from all sources is critical, and analyzing why legislators or constituents do what they do, what motivates them, what constituent constraints may exist is in many cases just as important as gathering and analyzing the factual data and information.

Devouring the Resources

Starting each day during the legislative session requires well-disciplined focus and teamwork by Rifkin and his staff:

As the eyes and ears for the client, we have to be able to use our judgment and common sense in analyzing material and information from all sources. We devour newspapers. By nine o'clock, we have usually read the newspapers: *The Baltimore Sun*, *The Washington Post*, *The Annapolis Capital*, *The Daily Record*, and the business journals. We also subscribe to a clipping service that gives us newspapers from around the state. The clipping results are delivered to us each morning with tabs in it and notes to send to specific clients. We also have our own in-house clipping operation, one of the things we do first thing in the morning. We cut through and use our time most efficiently. We read trade journals and review committee files. If there is information that is direct or tangential that we can lay our hands on from the clients or the institutions themselves, then we do so. As information becomes available, it is catalogued, filed on computer for later retrieval, and distributed to our clients for comments and review. On a daily basis, information is faxed each morning to our clients who in turn keep us up to date on changing trends. Again, this helps to lay the foundation for what later will be the important process of analysis, advocacy, and education.

We have to know at all times what legislation affects our clients, and therefore, we rely on our updated statutes. We get the daily electronic synopsis of new legislation through the Maryland Legislative Information Service, early in the morning, track amendments and rule changes by computer feed, and profile each client's status each day. After that's all been roughed out, we take a look at what the general hearing schedule is for the day to try and manage this proliferation of information and make it work for us as opposed to working against us.

Critical Success Factors: Relevant Information Resources Combined with Technology and Human Expertise

Critical success factors in Rifkin's office include resources mentioned above as well as the following elements—relevant information resources, technology, and human expertise:
1. *Relevant Information Resources.*
   - Online, up-to-the-minute state legislative information: The Maryland Legislative Information System (MLIS) is the online version of Maryland's General Assembly's Department of Legislative Reference Bill Status System (now with a homepage for public access at http://mlis.state.md.us/). It is available to every citizen of Maryland. Information in the Maryland General Assembly homepage comes from the Senate and House floors and from the committees. It is this information that is critical to all legislators, lobbyists, and interested citizens during the legislative process.

      The MLIS is where Rifkin monitors the legislative process for up-to-the-minute changes that include current information on:
      - House and Senate proceedings
      - Bill information and status
      - Status of bills and their profile

      Rifkin and his staff disseminate the current information on bills and their status to clients. (Note: Access to MLIS is free, but for up-to-the-minute status information, there is an annual subscription fee.)
   - Commercial online databases of regional, national, international, legislative and business information: The commercial online database, LEXIS-NEXIS (http://www.lexis.com) is used by Rifkin's staff. Here are found

federal materials, legislative information, agency decisions, government procurement, state materials, and news from around the world. Rifkin says they don't need a physical library, because there's nothing they can't get online.

• Other resources:
In addition to the resources used daily as noted above, Rifkin's staff uses other standard legal reference resources, electronic tools, and services to enhance the information-gathering and disseminating process.

■ *The Annotated Code of Maryland*, Michie Publications, Charlottesville, VA (http://www.michie. com). This is the standard reference resource utilized throughout the legislative process by all legislators. It provides a topical arrangement of all state-codified statutes, i.e., in subjects such as agriculture, environment, transportation, labor, insurance, health care, and many more. It is approximately 20-30 volumes and is supplemented each year.

■ *The Maryland Manual*, available through Maryland's State Archives in electronic format at http://www.mdarchives.state.md and also in print format. It provides an overview of the organizational structure and staffing of Maryland government.

■ The Internet has opened up many resources that were not previously available. Additional resources Rifkin will be using more in the future are the websites that provide links to legislative information services in other states.

■ Trade associations are also considered a good resource for information on businesses and specific industry sectors.

2. *Technology*
Rifkin and his partners know that using information technologies is crucial for them to stay ahead of the competition, and more importantly, to put themselves in a position to be leaders. "We have done that since day one," says Rifkin.

He explains that the staff (in the Baltimore and Annapolis offices) consists of nine attorneys, two legislative assistants, one computer assistant, and four secretaries.

They have learned how lean and efficient technology can be. They are now able to perform with half the number because of the technologies...and do it in such a way that they don't miss a step while gathering and disseminating information.

Technology resources used include the following:

- The communication system: This consists of a broadcast fax system that on any given day will transmit dozens of current legislative hearing notices, clippings from relevant newspaper or magazine articles, and ongoing developments between lawyer and client. "This labor-saving technology allows the staff to program and send faxes to clients at specific times so that they don't have to stand next to the fax machine feeding paper into it, thus saving time so that we can go home at night and be with our families," says Rifkin.
- The dictation system: The Dictaphone "Straight Talk" Digital Voice Delivery System allows the staff to dictate a letter or memo from anywhere in the world and send it directly to their office for transcription, allowing for instant updates to client's communications.
- Home office access: What ultimately ties this operation together is that in every lawyer's home are a computer and a fax machine, so there is a direct link between all of the systems and the individuals who are working on a specific case. "It is beneficial. On a snowy day, not only can we be productive, we can gain some efficiencies," Rifkin says.

Rifkin's long-range view is that there is a lessening need, ultimately, for square footage and office space but a continuing need for interface between individuals and information:

> In our view, we can reduce our needs for hard physical space as we increase the productivity through the technologies we use. For example, we now take laptops to all legislative sessions, and we can make immediate changes from our screens and mail the

documents back to the office or to our clients to keep
them up to date with ongoing developments.

3. *Human Expertise*
    •   Analysis, presentation, and advocacy: Rifkin believes
        that the information itself simply represents the raw
        materials.

> The purpose for which lawyers are hired is for their
> ability to analyze the raw data...to make sense of the
> information, to present, and to advocate on behalf of
> one's clients using the information as a resource, all of
> which is a function of experience and a function of the
> knowledge base one has.

Perhaps most importantly, it is who you know. "The legislative
process is still a people-to-people business," says Rifkin. "The technology
provides quick access to resources from which to make logical, common-
sense, practical decisions. It saves time so there is more time to talk to
people and to make decisions."

Notes

1.   Tom Johnson, "Assembly: A Pivotal Session for Business, Legislative
Session Will Test Glendening's Pledge to Aid Biz," *Warfield's Business Record,*
Monday, 8 January 1996.

Chapter 3 A Corporate Information Gatekeeper

Steven L. Lubetkin

> Research into the theories of communications processes in technology back in the 1970s developed the concept of technological "gatekeepers," i.e., people who seem to have most contact with other members of the group and who function as informal information disseminators.
>
> Thomas J. Allen, *Managing the Flow of Technology*, 1977

Through strategic use of Internet resources, I have now become a de facto information expert on behalf of analysts and executives for Standard & Poor's Ratings Services," says Steven Lubetkin, who directs the international rating agency's research library. This information gathering and disseminating power places Lubetkin in a role of information "gatekeeper" within the corporation. The underlying concept, originally referring to scientists and engineers in academic environments, proposes that gatekeepers are people who have the most contact with other members of the group and who function as informal information disseminators.

Lubetkin's gatekeeper function also involves monitoring, like a sentinel watching for gathering clouds and warning signals from the outside environment, while being attuned at all times to his internal environment. And when credit analysts at Standard & Poor's need information about their subjects, they often call or see Lubetkin.

Steven Lubetkin is, in many ways, a model knowledge worker, for he has the technological know-how, the communications expertise, the business education, the learned sense of the specialized information needs of his unit, and the (de facto) authority to exercise his expertise and to get the job done.

Guerilla Technology

Lubetkin has been doing what he calls "guerilla technology" for a number of years. As an enthusiastic adopter of computer technology in the early eighties, he explains how there was talk then about mini-computers being the wave of the future, and how it was a radical notion that the CEO of any company should even sit down at a computer:

> When I started getting involved in the technology (before PCs), I'd sit down at the terminal and get teased unmercifully by colleagues who would walk by and say, "Oh look at the new secretary" (it was very politically incorrect of them). At the time, word processing and computer terminals were seen very much as a secretarial tool, not one that professionals used. Instead, we would sit in our cubicles and type at a typewriter, or write our drafts on legal pads and hand them to a secretary who would then type our notes and hand us back a printed copy. It was very inefficient.

Self-Taught Information Skills

Self-taught computer skills also led Lubetkin to online databases in their early years of development. "At the time, the electronic resources that were available were DIALOG® and LEXIS-NEXIS, and they were very expensive," he says. When CompuServe and Dow Jones News Retrieval started to come to the surface, Lubetkin got involved in using them. He says that "people who paid the bills didn't understand it, and until you could show the value of the information, you had to pull the data into the organization." He took a chance and bought a few introductory subscriptions to the commercial databases. He started learning to use them, getting data that he passed on to the people he worked with and asking them: "Is this the kind of information that would be useful to you?" And they would say, "Wow," or "Yeah," or "This is very interesting." Subsequently, Lubetkin started searching on a more regular basis, providing more and more information.

Gaining Credibility

A solid grounding in journalism, public relations, and media relations (crisis communications) served Lubetkin well when he was originally hired in 1991 by Standard & Poor's to write speeches and articles for senior executives within the company. And it was these skills combined with his "guerilla" techniques for using technologies to find information that influenced his being promoted to organize and manage seminars, programs, and conferences on financial market subjects as well as to help Standard & Poor's credit and bond analysts prepare seminar presentations for their clientele.

Examples of current seminars include such specialized titles as "Asset-Backed Securitization," "Real Estate Finance," and "Municipal Ratings/Latin America." Outside conferences at which S&P people speak have included a global business research subprime conference: "Credit Scoring and Risk-Based Pricing," and fixed income daily conference: "Bond Market Impacts of California's Prop 218."

Now Providing Financial Information and Services to 80 Countries

Lubetkin explains that the corporate clientele who attend the credit ratings seminars are "financial intermediaries, investment bankers, brokers, and anyone who is involved in the issuance of bonds or debt securities, or in the investment of those securities, such as portfolio managers and institutional investors, and who need to understand ratings. They want to meet with the analysts or they want to meet with other participants in the market to compare notes."

In addition to the in-house seminars for clients, credit rating tele-conferences are now offered and are growing in number. Lubetkin reports that clients using conference calls totaled 5,500 worldwide in 1996. "It is 'incredible' how much time it saves and the exchanges of information that can take place," says Lubetkin." For the Seminars homepage, go to http://www.ratings.standardpoor.com/seminars.

The Role of Credit Ratings
in the World of Finance

Standard & Poor's Ratings Services is a division of the McGraw Hill Companies, Inc., an information content company comprised of information and media services, financial services, and educational and professional publications. It is within Ratings Services that bond and credit analysts monitor and analyze the credit quality of nearly $10 trillion worth of bonds and other financial instruments. This includes ratings on more than 30,000 bonds and preferred stock issues of some 5,600 companies in North America, Europe, Japan, and Australia, more than 13,000 municipal, state, sovereign, and supranational entities, and 10,000 structured debt issues.

The Industrial Revolution and
Credit Ratings

Standard & Poor's roots formed during Civil War days when railroads were the principal engine propelling the Industrial Revolution and investors needed assessments of railroad finance and credit. The recognizable Standard & Poor's letter grade ratings symbols (AAA to D) go back to 1916. These ratings are highly significant, because a company's creditworthiness is a key investment decision tool in the world of business.

The Standard & Poor's credit rating process involves extensive qualitative, quantitative, and legal analysis, as well as constant monitoring of the leading financial and monetary indicators that drive complex credit markets. To see Standard & Poor's Ratings Criteria, go to http://www. ratings.standardpoor.com/criteria/index.htm.

The Information Factory

Standard & Poor's Ratings Services has become a veritable information factory, employing professional credit analysts whose

information activities are organized in departments along the lines of
issuer types including:

- *Corporate Finance.* Includes long-term debt, commercial
  paper, preferred stock and public/private placements in the
  areas of industrial, natural resources, utilities, transportation,
  and retailers.
- *Financial Institutions.* Rates the creditworthiness of banks,
  finance companies, savings and loans, brokerage firms, and
  money market and mutual bond funds.
- *Insurance Rating Services.* Includes bonds and commercial
  paper and the claims-paying ability of insurance companies.
- *Municipal Finance.* Rates debt of state and local governments,
  and public authorities, such as government-owned utilities,
  educational and health care facilities, housing agencies, public
  transportation systems, and other tax-exempt obligors.

The Evolution of a Gatekeeper's Role

Steven Lubetkin's role in this information factory as a director in
global ratings development under Standard & Poor's Ratings Services has
evolved from writing corporate speeches to information gatekeep-
er/disseminator, to organizing and now directing ratings seminars,
research, teleconferencing, and customer service. Most recently, as
methods of delivery of information have expanded and the demand for
information resources of all kinds have increased within his own unit,
Lubetkin is taking on even more information responsibilities.

For instance, in 1996, Lubetkin assumed responsibility for the
ratings library (previously housed in the equity side of Standard &
Poor's). He is now guiding the development of this "new" library service
within Ratings Services. Because there is less space available for collections (i.e., print) or for tables and chairs for reading or browsing, the
library is moving more toward electronic storage, retrieval, and dissemination of information to Standard & Poor's analysts. In fact, few people
come into the "actual" library, and most of the requests from analysts and
clients are handled via e-mail, fax, or phone from their desktop. The
library now uses CD-ROM, commercial online databases, and the Internet
to answer client questions, and there is a reference librarian from the
original library who helps Lubetkin utilize these resources and provides
research support.

The Internet:
A New Force to be Reckoned With

The Internet is becoming a key medium for communicating, accessing, and delivering information both inside the group and to the outside world. Here, Lubetkin monitors discussion lists, news sources, and business publications, and finds the business intelligence-gathering results especially satisfactory. He reports that he spends "a couple of hours a day" on the Internet monitoring and checking for information, answering questions, and sending information to those who need it (see For More Information, Internet Resources Used by Steve Lubetkin).

The Standard & Poor's Ratings Services homepage (http://www.ratings.standardpoor.com) Lubetkin is helping to develop is now considered a key corporatewide medium for information activities of all sorts, including communicating with Standard & Poor's clients. In Lubetkin's area of seminars and teleconferences, the webpage works well for disseminating information about the ratings seminars and provides ease of access for seminar schedules and bios, as well as a place to order tapes of the seminars. There will no doubt be many more applications and uses for Global Ratings Services as the World Wide Web develops.

A New Kind of Knowledge Worker

There is no formal job title to describe Lubetkin's kind of knowledge work. His combined skill sets and knowledge bases are unique and varied. He has had long-term direct access to and experience with information resources both within and without the corporation, and extensive, close communication with information users (both analysts and corporate clients). He understands the technology needed to access and deliver information, and he is extremely knowledgeable about the specific content (meaning) of his information. He has a grasp of the big picture and as a generalist knows the issues and activities within his own groups and what information is needed to answer their questions.

Lubetkin's current job incorporates an important strategic role that is now emerging in many companies and organizations, i.e., making best use of the company's capital assets—the information bases and knowledge of its own people. This can ultimately lead to quality decisions and revenue for the company.

For More Information

Internet Resources Used by Steven Lubetkin

Lubetkin uses the Internet for a wide range of business, financial, and economic research on behalf of analysts and executives at Standard & Poor's Ratings Services. Following are some of the Internet resources and applications that he has documented:

- Federal budget via Internet: While attending a municipal housing seminar in Phoenix, Lubetkin learned that the Federal budget was being released via Internet. Using a laptop PC in his hotel room, he logged into a commercial Internet provider and downloaded the entire budget, then printed relevant chapters for the director of government relations at Standard & Poor's to review.
- Business Sources on the Internet: A homepage describing a wide range of business reference sources on the Internet.
- BUSLIB-L: An Internet discussion group about business libraries that he uses frequently.
- Congressional Directory obtained via FTP.
- Telephone conference calls: Lubetkin's group participates in a number of conference calls using an MCI conference call service; MCI sends the attendance list to his mailbox via MCI Mail over the Internet. He can then distribute the list to the participants via e-mail, and save a significant amount of paper distribution.
- Cryptography: Following discussions of cryptographic policy and trends in data security via news groups, host files, and other resources; sharing information with information management and legal departments.
- Discussions with Federal Energy Regulatory Commission (FERC) making rulings accessible via Internet for utility analysts.
- Economic resources on the Internet: Lubetkin distributes documents to various people within his group.
- FCC cable TV rate decision and actions: Lubetkin retrieved the government document and e-mailed it to the ratings analysts covering the cable and telecommunications industry within an hour after the decisions were issued.
- GOVDOC-L postings: Internet discussion about government documents and research materials.
- Health Security Act, full text of legislation: Text obtained via Internet and E-mailed to analysts.

- India: Used Internet to obtain *CIA World Book of Facts* which contains information about countries, as well as State Department reports, other countries' news, and discussion group information.
- Internet Legal Resources document: E-mailed to Standard & Poor's legal department.
- Juris Database: FOIA request denied by Department of Justice: DOJ decision letter obtained via Internet, copy sent to Standard Poor's Legal Department.
- NAFTA: Complete text of NAFTA obtained via Internet e-mailed to analysts interested in the topic as it relates to their credit analysis.
- RiskNET: Internet discussion about risk management and insurance issues, being distributed to Insurance Department.
- RISKS: Internet news group on computer security issues, e-mailed to Standard & Poor's information management and legal departments.
- VIRUS-L Internet discussion on computer viruses: Distributed FAQ (Frequently Asked Questions) document to managers in information management.
- White House texts: Receives regular notification via Internet e-mail of White House transcripts and position papers available; requests and obtains full-text documents via e-mail for distribution to key analysts.

Notes

1.   Standard & Poor's Rating Services Seminars and Teleconferences Homepage, "Calendar of Events," at http://www.ratings.standardpoor.com/ seminars.

Chapter 4 An Information Technology Consultant

Samuel B. Hopkins

There is a world market for about five computers.
Thomas J. Watson, Sr. (spoken in 1943),
in Cerf and Navasky, *The Experts Speak*, 1984

Perhaps Thomas Watson,[1] founder and first president of IBM, was a bit shortsighted when he said that there really wasn't much of a market for computers, or maybe he was reflecting the technothink theory of his day. But there can be no doubt now that the growth of computer technology over the past 30 years has changed the world as we once knew it.

In 1984, after a career change from public health to private law practice (he graduated from Harvard Law School), Sam Hopkins decided to take advantage of his combined technical and legal expertise to build a business that would help law firms use the then new business tool called the "microcomputer." Since then, he has worked with law firms as a consultant who advises on computer system evaluation, selection, and implementation. In particular, he helps with case management, time-keeping, billing, word processing, legal research, and electronic access to state court systems.

Hopkins and other consultants like him play a major role in selecting new technology for law firms. The service most requested of Hopkins is help with timekeeping and billing software. Next is networking of computers, and the third is help with general ledger and related accounting software. Hopkins believes that his services help clients avoid misallocation of time, labor, and funds by having one "general contractor" to implement all the basic technologies within the office. This includes planning, negotiation with vendors, project management, purchasing, installation, training, troubleshooting, and ongoing support.

Setting High Standards for Research

It is essential for Hopkins to have access to information in order to serve his client base, and he utilizes many of the research skills he learned in law school and in public health to find and use information. Since doing demographic and behavioral research he conducted in villages in Pakistan while working with family planning programs, Hopkins has set high standards for obtaining accurate and relevant information. "Ideally, the literature I choose to search should include results of empirical research that meet the standards of good science," says Hopkins.

Keeping informed on computer technology is a challenge, he admits. The field is changing as fast as any field of knowledge. This means not only that he must acquire new knowledge at a constant and high rate, but that any knowledge or skill may become obsolete before he can use it to his or his clients' advantage. This problem puts a premium on the need to acquire and use information efficiently. "If I know where I can find information quickly, I can postpone getting it until there is a direct use [for the information] for a particular client," Hopkins says. This is analogous to the "just in time" purchasing of parts that lowers manufacturing costs. Nevertheless, Hopkins must still continuously gather many kinds of information in his field.

Defining the Role of the Gatherer/
User of Information

Is Hopkins an "end user" of information or an "information provider/specialist"? He furnishes his own interpretation and says that many times the roles overlap and that "we can all wear more than one hat." He says that when he is *preparing* to make recommendations to his clients, i.e., when he is in the data and information gathering mode, he is an end user because he is gathering data and information for his own needs. But in *presenting* his recommendations (usually face to face) to his clients, he becomes an information provider/specialist, because he has added value through synthesizing, analyzing, and applying his own judgment and opinion on the subject and then communicating it to the client.

How Hopkins Gathers and Uses Information

Technology for Retrieving and Storing Personal Knowledge Bases. Hopkins maintains paper files and indexes publications in his personal library, and he also accumulates annotated directories of information from all sources described below. The computer he uses to maximize efficiency in adding to his knowledge base is a Prolinear 1.5 lb. "palmbook" computer. "This palmbook," he says, "is a very unusual, little-known model that, unlike other palmbooks, uses regular desktop software. It also allows touch typing, because it is 9.5 inches wide instead of only 6-8 inches like all the 'palmbooks' that are widely advertised and available from mass merchandisers. It can use 'flashcard, solid-state devices that store up to 160 megabytes of programs and data without a hard drive." Because of its size and convenience of use, Hopkins carries his own knowledge base in this small computer at all times so that he can recall any support information he may need while he is meeting with a client.

Person-to-Person Networking. Hopkins uses an extensive network of colleagues to gather information, compare notes, and help understand how better to communicate with his own clients. Most frequently he confers with a Seattle-based consultant, and over the years, they have shared the task of researching new products and upgrades. He makes the point that colleagues who do not compete, because of geographical distances, are more inclined to share their knowledge, and this relationship helps Hopkins to update his knowledge quickly when he receives a request for help from a client. Since these consultants work solo and have few employees, this cooperation permits each to operate as what some now call a "virtual corporation," i.e., they can operate with the knowledge resources of a much larger business entity, but with much lower overhead. This in turn allows hourly fees that are more affordable than those charged by the larger consulting firms that specialize in the legal market.

Customers Are Key. One of his most important information resources is his customers. Because they are close to the everyday work environment, "customers are the most vital source of information about what you should be doing," Hopkins says. "We should be listening more often to what they want and what they need."

The Importance of Trade and Association Conferences. Current information also comes from attending conferences, trade shows, professional meetings, and related events. Hopkins attends the following conferences as often as he can:

- Annual Meetings of the American Bar Association (ABA) and the Maryland Bar Association (MBA)
- TechShow, the American Bar Association, Law Practice Management Section
- Legal Tech, a trade show

The Printed Word: Magazines and Newsletters. Hopkins subscribes to specialized periodicals that deal exclusively with lawyers and/or computers, along with several that target small businesses. He says that he is not wedded to these resources and that he constantly evaluates their value, which changes every year. Most of these resources are now also available on the Internet. Following are his descriptions of some key resources he is currently using (for contact information, see For More Information):

- *InfoWorld* is a tabloid-sized publication that provides a solid overview of new technology, along with insider industry news not found in other publications. This is where I get some of my most essential news. *InfoWorld* is especially helpful in providing early warnings about problems in each version of DOS, Windows, OS/2, word processing software, and other mass market products. The publication is not afraid to anger Microsoft, WordPerfect, Novell, and other major advertisers by giving negative test results or reporting the negative comments it receives from subscribers.
- *Law Technology Product News*, an affiliate of the *National Law Journal*, is compiled from vendor press releases. It showcases dozens of products of high practical value to lawyers, from scanning software to CD-ROM libraries to notebook computers. Because of its currency of sources, it has the shortest lead time of any of the publications I read. Its strength is its focus on lawyers' needs. Also, it is perfectly suited to quick scanning.
- *PC Magazine* is arguably the computer industry's highest profile publication. Its test reports are essential. *PC Magazine* tests are more thorough than those done by other magazines, and it invariably tests more products than its competitors do. I recommend many products (notebook computers, for example) to clients based on the test ratings in *PC Magazine*.

- In addition, there are several newsletters of the American Bar Association Law Practice Management Section such as *Lawyering Tools and Techniques, Counselor's Computer & Management Report, Law Practice Today,* and *Law Practice Management.* In the last, G. Burgess Allison's technical update column is a highlight. I think Allison's irreverence and humor can help reduce lawyers' anxiety about the vast scope and complexity of technology. For example, Allison points out that vendors have pressured attorneys (and everyone else) to buy "software suites" either by packaging them with hardware or offering deep discounts. These are overwhelming to most users and, without guidance, will demoralize many of them. The promotions imply that if we are not using the whole suites and at least a good portion of the thousands of functions, we are novices. But the truth is different and Allison tells it like it is.

Electronic Resources: Online Databases, CD-ROM, and the Internet

Online Databases. There are a number of reasons Hopkins is beginning to recognize the valuable potential of electronic resources, e.g., commercial online systems, CD-ROM, and the Internet. One is that technology information becomes obsolete so quickly that saving it in hard (print) copy is not justified. Another reason is that there is not enough space to continually accumulate and save printed resources.

Hopkins' priority now is to minimize the time he spends reading and researching "just in case" computer applications, when a client is not paying for it at least a part of the time. So, he has increased his use of online databases and CD-ROMs to find focused information, citations to the literature, and full text of articles that could enhance, supplement, or replace printed resources. Here are a few of the electronic resources Hopkins uses:

- Hopkins occasionally uses CompuServe's *Legal Forum (LAWSIG,* http://www.compuserve.com/world/articles/forum. html) "to sample how the online exchange of information can be a cost effective tool for an attorney's practice," he says. "It also gives examples of how online forums and discussion groups operate."

- One of the nonlaw, computer technology related databases Hopkins uses is created by Ziff Publications, which publishes *PC Magazine* and other computer periodicals. Hopkins can now access these publications through the World Wide Web at ZiffNet (http://www.ziffnet.com).

CD-ROM. "The options for information resources on CD-ROM are growing exponentially in every field of specialization," Hopkins says. In the areas of law, Hopkins mentions West Publications (see For More Information). He cites one of the major CD-ROMs for computer information, *Computer Select,* where subscribers receive a monthly CD-ROM that contains the full text of many computer-related periodicals published during that year.

The Internet. Hopkins is not a constant user of the Internet. But he does particularly recommend a site now on the Internet called Counsel Connect as an invaluable tool for communicating with experts, sending e-mail, discussion groups, and doing research about many legal and technology issues. However, he cautions, "You can gather too much information. Part of the problem in gathering and utilizing information is that we spend too much time receiving and processing information that we never intended to look for, simply because it is in the periodicals that come in our daily mail. And this is certainly true of the Internet."

Questioning the Productivity of Computers

While Hopkins has spent time browsing the Internet, he questions its productivity for finding and locating information, at least for now. In fact, most recently he has begun shifting his priorities toward the overall question of productivity of computer use. He cites what he considers a seminal book on the issue, *The Trouble with Computers, Usefulness, Usability, and Productivity,*[2] by Thomas K. Landauer, professor of psychology and fellow of the Institute of Cognitive Science at the University of Colorado, who explains the trouble with computers:

> The situation sums up this way. Computers are often used to do things that are irrelevant or detrimental to true productivity, such as purely share-shifting marketing functions or excess report generation. And when computer applications are intended to increase worker or process efficiency, they often don't help. There are chicken-and-egg dynamics here. In the business climate of the last few decades, managers have been so interested in short-term market share that they

have not devoted needed resources to making computers do better things. But also it has proved so much harder to make computers do serious work that they have been diverted to easier but more frivolous employment. In either case, we need to make computers into much better tools for work, both for the work of individuals and for the work or organizations. When good tools become available, their use for productivity enhancement will be a potent competitive weapon and will supplant, or at least supplement, unproductive uses.[3]

In the future, Hopkins wants to help his clients apply the solutions recommended by Landauer, who calls them the three "UCDs": user-centered design (user task analysis, evaluation, and testing), user-centered development (identifying the testers and the users), and user-centered deployment (what to use computers for and how).

Since there are so few who appear to share Landauer's and Hopkins' views on "the trouble with computers," Hopkins says that he needs help finding them. He believes that the Internet may prove to be invaluable in this regard and also in adding converts to the cause.

How Hopkins Archives and Retrieves Information

Making the transition from paper to electronic information will foster new technologies and skills for finding, organizing, and retrieving electronic information. For example, Hopkins explains that many times, consultants might find some bit of data that could be useful but have no system for organizing this information. "In fact," Hopkins says, "many consultants end up with an unorganized, inefficient work environment, where articles languish unread in piles on floor or tables, and boxes of new software sit unopened on shelves. Unwilling or unable to deal with the unending 'information explosion,' many simply try to keep a small part of their knowledge updated and ignore the rest."

"What will happen when electronic information piles up 'high' in computers and e-mail networks? It is easy to be right back to the problem that caused you to go online in the first place, which was accumulating more information than you can process, store and retrieve at an affordable cost," says Hopkins. "Now you will be running out of disk space or accumulating too many CDs. So then you must climb another learning curve, adopting new technology and procedures for archiving information and retrieving it (not necessarily to change but just to get the information)."

Using Brute Force

Hopkins suggests that one of the ways small law firms can keep their data organized and retrievable without spending tens of thousands of dollars is by using a "brute force" program that searches and retrieves the full text of all information on a hard disk or CD-ROM. There are a number of excellent products on the market. He suggests ZyIndex (Zylab, Arlington Heights, Illinois) for legal specialty storage and organization and OmniPage (Caere's OCR Software) for text and image scanning. This product is especially good for major litigation.

Notes

1.   Christopher Cerf and Victor Navasky, *The Experts Speak* (New York: Random House, 1994).
2.   Thomas K. Landauer, *The Trouble with Computers, Usefulness, Usability, and Productivity* (Cambridge, MA: MIT Press, 1996).
3.   Ibid, 136.

For More Information

Hopkins's selected information resources for advising law firms on law office technology and management:

•   Trade and Association Conferences

TechShow (Association)
American Bar Association
Law Practice Management Section
750 N. Lake Shore Drive
Chicago, IL 60601
312/988-5619
http://www.techshow.com/

Legal Tech (Trade)
111 Central Park West
New York, NY 10023
212/877-5619
http://www.legaltechcpi.com/

Print Resources (including WWW sites)

InfoWorld (The voice of personal computing in the enterprise)
InfoWorld Publishing Company
155 Bovet Road, Suite 800
San Mateo, CA 94402
415/572 7341
http://www.inforworld.com

Law Technology Product News (Products, systems and services for
law firms)
New York Law Publishing Company
345 Park Avenue South
New York, NY 10010
111 Eighth Avenue, Suite 900
New York, NY 10011
1-800/888-8300
http://www.ljx.com/lptn

PC Magazine, The Independent Guide to Personal Computing
Ziff Davis Publishing Co.
Onc Park Avenue
New York, NY 10016-5802
1-800/289-0429
http://www.zdnet.com

Law Practice Management (Section of Law Practice Management,
American Bar Association)
Law Practice Management
C/O American Bar Association
750 N. Lake Shore Drive
Chicago, IL 60611
http://www.abanet.org/lpm/home.html

American Bar Association Journal
American Bar Association
750 N. Lake Shore Drive
Chicago, IL 60611
http://www.abanet.org/journal/home.html

• Electronic Databases

Ziff Publications on CompuServe
Telephone: 1-800/848-8199
http://www.compuserve.com
or
http://www.zdnet.com

The Legal Forum on CompuServe (LAWSIG)
Telephone: 1-800/848-8199
http://www.compuserve.com/world/articles/forum.html

• CD-ROM

West Publications
http://www.westpub.com
Computer Select
1-800/419-0313
http://www.online-info.com/info-access/compsel.htm

Chapter 5   An Investment Advisor

Barbara E. Doty

> Professional investors are heavy users of information...information is
> power up to a point...until the abundance of information available is
> so excessive as to be overpowering.
>
> John Bogle, *Bogle on Mutual Funds, New Perspectives*
> *for the Intelligent Investor*, 1994

President and chief investment officer of the Baltimore company Majority Asset Management, Inc. Barbara Doty knows information overload pressure well. With a goal of providing her clients "investment advisory services with a personal touch," Doty handles most of the research, client service, portfolio management, and marketing for the company.

Working independently for five years without the help of an in-house research staff, Doty has managed what many money managers cannot: to keep up with the tremendous flow of information about financial markets and to convert information into successful investments. "Information is a hundred percent of what I do," says Doty. "Without it, I couldn't make any investment judgments. It has infinite value to me."

From Big Business to Her Own Business

A veteran of the financial world, an MBA and a Certified Financial Analyst (CFA), the highly articulate Doty worked her way up from a summer job in the research department of Wall Street investment firm Goldman Sachs, and then through several major investment firms: Bankers' Trust, Alex Brown & Sons (as a principal in the private client division), and Kidder Peabody Asset Management as senior vice president and member of the board of directors. She has a reputation for being a driven worker, and she's still remembered at Alex Brown as the woman who returned to work three days after childbirth.

Avoiding Popular Delusions
and the Madness of Crowds

Doty is an individualist who operates with a unique style. She is wary of ways in which the corporate herd instinct can affect analyses of the market. The bottom line for her isn't necessarily what the numbers and statistics show; it's people's *perceptions* of this information. "I am passionate about knowing what other people think. A lot of what prove to be successful investments and acceptable ideas to investors is a function of what people are hearing or appear to believe," says Doty. She says, "I really want to know what the influences are on people's behavior, how they spend their money, whether they are buying clothes or houses, whether they're spending or saving money, whether they feel secure in their jobs, or whether they plan to travel, because that suggests that where they spend their time and money will lead to successful investments."

The First Layer of Reading:
The Daily News

Following public perceptions in financial matters is a many-layered process. The first step for Doty, and typically her first duty of the day, is to sample a handful of the high-circulation newspapers that inform the general public: the *New York Times*, the *Wall Street Journal, Investor's*

Daily, the *Washington Post*, the *Baltimore Sun*, the *New York Daily News*, and the *New York Post*, "I'm addicted to that morning reading," she says.

The Second Layer:
Wall Street Analysts' Reports

The information necessary to create an accurate picture of people's perceptions about the marketplace is however significantly different from what is needed to follow the market itself. Doty initially bypasses companies' annual reports and the hard numbers that a lot of money managers use to determine the stability of a company. "I don't like to do the frontline work," she says, "It's more useful after somebody else has pored through all those little bits and pieces of things. I don't like going through the raw data."

Instead, Doty turns to secondary interpretation from Wall Street analysts, reports that she can access as a result of her trading relationships with investment banks, consulting organizations, or research firms. These reports provide in-depth research results on a company or industry that might include a discussion of the investment thesis, or industry statistics, prospects, and expectations for growth. Or it might provide a breakdown of company operations, the outlook for the industry, a review of recent events, and a view of the strategic goals for each division of the company. This quality research is invaluable for Doty's investment decision-making process.

Doty finds Wall Street analysts who cover her companies and industries though "word of mouth," or sometimes in *Nelson's Directory of Investment Research*.[1] She also reads the *Institutional Investor*,[2] which keeps a close eye on Wall Street firms and publishes a popular annual list of "all-star" research analysts.

Next Stop: Mass Market Wisdom,
Psycho Babble and Hot Shots

Doty next pays attention to resources that provide insight into what the mass markets of investors are taking in as today's investment wisdom, resources such as Lou Rukeyser's *Wall Street Newsletter*[3] and the

television show *Wall Street Week,*[4] which he hosts. "I'm interested in what
people who are perceived to be smart investors are doing and what they're
thinking," says Doty. "I'm always interested in what George Soros
(Quantum Fund) is doing. I'm interested in Mario Gabelli (Gabelli &
Co.), Lee Cooperman (Omega Partners), and Warren Buffet (Berkshire
Hathaway) as well. It doesn't mean that I can implement their investment
philosophies, I just want to know what they are thinking, as well as what
they think is attractive (or isn't attractive). That gives me things to think
about that I can apply in my own areas."

Other Resources

Other tools Doty calls the "technical derivatives" of monitoring
expertise are the charts. She says these give her a different way of
assessing what she has read and how that can affect the behavior of
stocks. Among those she uses are William O'Neil's Daily Graph,[5]
Mansfield's Charts,[6] Ed Noonan's *Contradvisory Report,*[7] and Ed Hyman
at International Strategy and Investment Group (ISI).[8]

Although Doty values the opinion of insiders, one of her most
important resources is available in the typical grocery store aisle: *Money*
magazine. "It's a very interesting blend of market savvy and psychology,"
says Doty. "It's a consumer-oriented publication, but it also has elements
of the investment process. The *Wall Street Journal* or *Investor's Daily* are
more finely tuned, but they run deep and narrow."

Investmentthink and
How to Read Between the Lines

The key to getting pertinent information out of such a mass of
material—Doty claims that she spends about six hours of every day just
reading—is to start with the right focus. "What I focus on in my reading
are the concepts," she states. "I don't concentrate on what did so and so
earn last year, the year before, or the year before that. Unless I own a
specific stock or I'm definitely planning to buy a specific stock, what I'm
initially looking for are concepts, trends, theories, market positions,
strategies—things that are easier to retain."

Doty feels that it's also important to understand that the best thing to look for often isn't explicitly stated in the texts one reads. "To get at the investment-think that drives market players, you have to read between the lines. To go from the text of what people are saying to 'Do I buy this or not?' requires that you derive a meaning that someone else does not," she says. "In the investment process, you're thinking about the big picture as well as individual company issues. You're thinking about the global marketplace, the U.S. market relative to other markets, your industries versus other industries, your companies versus other companies. There's hardly a piece of information that you can just throw away."

Person to Person

After compiling and sorting through the secondhand data she retrieves through the media, Doty often goes directly to the company, where she talks to the CEO, the CFO, or the head of investor relations, the department set up specifically to talk with investment analysts. Or, she will ask to be invited to one of the company conferences. "But I want to ask questions in private," she says. "The only edge you have is your own analysis, and you shouldn't share it." To accomplish this task, Doty has become a notorious hardball questioner. "I rely heavily on my ability to get people to tell me things that they don't tell other people or to tell it to me in ways that they don't tell others," she claims.

"CEOs don't always give the best information," she observes. "Many times, I am more likely to ask questions of lower level people within the company, because they are less guarded, and you may get a different flavor. For example, I would go to a Toys-R-Us manager and ask 'What is selling or what isn't?'"

The Technological Aspect

Doty will be the first to admit that she's more comfortable dealing directly with people than finding the information she needs through computers. As a result of her lack of technological sophistication, she relies very little on the high-cost programs that bigger businesses use, and she frequently falls victim to the technophobia that many business people feel.

"You almost want to tell the software companies, don't bother to upgrade, because I've found my way around this program," says Doty, "Whatever it is I can't do now, I can live without it. Just don't make me learn something new!"

For most of her management needs, Doty uses a portfolio management program from Advent Software.[9] "It's a tool that many money managers use. I think it's a very well-designed program that can handle tons of portfolios, as well as a wide variety of securities."

Doty hasn't found consumer online databases all that relevant in the money management business. "Most databases give you detail about what happened 40 years ago, and that information isn't what compels me to buy or sell something. I am not very historically driven."

She does think there are things that might be useful on the Internet, but for her, it is not currently efficient.

This ahistorical mentality also carries over into print material. Don't look for libraries or stacks of old periodicals in Doty's office. "I'm not one of the world's big savers," she says, "I think information has a very finite life."

It's the Interpretation that Counts

Doty says that, in the end, "the only distinction any investment manager has is in the interpretation of the data and information that is gathered. It is having the skill to ask the different question, or being able to extrapolate a meaning from what is not said. If you're doing the right things, the results will show that over time."

Notes

1.   *Nelson's Directory of Wall Street Research* (212-484-4700)
2.   *Institutional Investor* (1-212-224-3233)
3.   Louis Rukeyser's *Wall Street Newsletter* (804-977-6600)
4.   *Wall Street Week* (410-356-5600)
5.   William O'Neil & Company, Inc. (http://www.dailygraphs.com or 310-448-6800)
6.   *Mansfield's Stock Charts* (201-795-0629)
7.   Contravisory Research Corp. (617-740-1786)
8.   International Strategy and Investment Group (ISI) (212-446-5600)

9.   Advent Software (1-800-678-7005)

For More Information

I.   The Chartered Financial Analyst (CFA) exam reflects the diverse, yet specialized information environment of the investment world. Barbara Doty's CFA designation places her among those in the investment community who have mastered a comprehensive and rigorous curriculum designed to reflect what is referred to by analysts as the current "body of knowledge" for the investment profession. In order to qualify for the program, administered through the Association for Investment Management and Research (AIMR), candidates are expected to demonstrate advanced levels of working knowledge of financial statement analysis, macro and micro-economics, and quantitative methods, as well as understanding of investment analysis and management, financial markets and instruments, fundamental investment valuation, and portfolio tools. For further information regarding the CFA exam and its courses of study, go to the AIMR homepage at http://www.aimr.org.

II.   Further reading on the subject of investing:

There are literally hundreds of books in any bookstore or library about the stock market and investments. The following is a list of those now considered classics that include advice from the experts or give historical perspective on the stock market.
   • *A Random Walk Down Wall Street* by Burton G. Malkiel (W.W. Norton, 1973). This author's thesis is that "a blind-folded monkey throwing darts at a newspaper's financial pages could select a portfolio that would do just as well as one carefully selected by the experts." Malkiel's experience in the money business, academia, and government lends credibility to his investment theories and approaches to the market.
   • *An Investor's Anthology*, edited by Charles D. Ellis (Dow-Jones Irwin, 1989). Excerpts from the literature of investing.
   • *Another Investor's Anthology*, edited by Charles D. Ellis (BusinessOne Irwin, 1991).

- *Barbarians at the Gate* by Bryan Burrough and Jouh Helyar (Harper & Row, 1990). A true best-seller of the late 80s, describing the excesses of the decade.
- *Bogle on Mutual Funds, New Perspectives for the Intelligent Investor* by John Bogle (Richard D. Irwin, 1994). A definitive book on mutual funds.
- *The Warren Buffet Way* by Robert Hagstron (Wiley, 1995). The financial genius of one of the world's wealthiest men who says, "It's easier to create wealth than to spend it."
- *Extraordinary Popular Delusions and the Madness of Crowds* by Charles Mackay (Harmon Books, 1980). While this was first published in 1841, it remains one of the most cited investment books in print for its numerous citations of crowd delusions throughout history.
- *The Money Game: "Adam Smith"* (Random House, 1968). The writer behind "Adam Smith," George J. W. Goodman is former editor of *Institutional Investor* and host of the PBS show "Adam Smith's Money World," who says: "If you don't know who you are, the stock market is an expensive place to find out."
- *One Up on Wall Street, How to Use What You Already Know to Make Money in the Market* by Peter Lynch. (Simon & Schuster, 1989). Classic stock tips from the former manager of the Fidelity Magellan Fund.
- *Beating the Street* by Peter Lynch (Simon & Schuster, 1993). More classic Peter Lynch.
- *Reminiscences of a Stock Operator* by Edwin Lefévre (1923). Written over 60 years ago, this is a fictionalized classic biography of a celebrated speculator who won and lost millions over the decades leading up to the crash of 1929. Losing all taught him how things work and what not to do.
- Graham and Dodd's *Security Analysis,* Fifth Edition, by Sidney Cottle, Roger F. Murray, and Frank E. Block (McGraw Hill, 1988). An investment classic on financial analysis, investment decision making, and security analysis.
- *Market Movers: A Complete Guide to Economic Statistics, Trends, Forces and News Events—and What They Mean to Your Investments* by Nancy Dunnan and Jay J. Pack (Warner Books, New York, 1993). A useful handbook that explains who and what moves the market.

- *The Money Masters* by John Train (Harper and Row, 1980) and *The New Money Masters: Winning Investment Strategies of Soros, Lynch, Steinhardt, Rogers, Neff, Wanger, Michaelis, and Carret* (Harper & Row, 1989). Profiles the experts of the 1980s.
- *Investment Gurus* by Peter J. Tenous (Simon & Schuster, 1996). Another batch of current Wall Street gurus.

III. "Information-Seeking Behavior of Securities Analysts: Individual and Institutional Influences, Information and Channels, and Outcomes" by Nancy Sadler Baldwin of Morgan Stanley and Co., Inc. and Ronald E. Rice, School of Communication, Information and Library Studies, Rutgers University (Journal of the American Society for Information Science, 48 [8], 1997: 674-693), provides important results of a study of securities analysts' information activities with conclusions that discuss the implications for securities analysts, institutional and retail investors, schools of library and information science, and practicing information professionals.

IV. Who Are the Experts?

Wall Street is replete with experts who come and go as "the Dow" rises and falls. An article from *Worth* magazine, "Who Really Moves the Market—The 50 People Investors Can't Afford to Ignore in 1995," by Ted Fishman and the editors, February 1995, lists the ever-changing roster of experts from year to year whose actions or ideas can create significant stock market activity.

1. Alan Greenspan, chairman of the Board of Governors of the Federal Reserve System
2. Hans Tietmeyer, president of the Bundesbank, German Central Bank
3. Bill Clinton, president of the United States
4. Newt Gingrich, representative from Georgia; Speaker of the House
5. Jeff Vinik, manager of Fidelity Magellan Fund
6. Yasuo Matsushita, chairman, Bank of Japan
7. Warren Buffet, chairman and CEO, Berkshire Hathaway, Inc.
8. Robert Rubin, secretary of the U.S. Treasury

9. Barton Biggs, chairman and CEO, Morgan Stanley Asset Management Co.
10. Peter Lynch, investor and author
11. Bill Gates, chairman and CEO, Microsoft Corp.
12. Charles S. Sanford Jr., CEO, Bankers Trust New York Corp.
13. George Soros, CEO, Soros Fund Management
14. John Neff, manager, Vanguard/Windsor Fund
15. Mark Holowesko, director of Global Equity Research, Templeton Worldwide, Inc.
16. John Meriwether, partner, Long Term Capital Management
17. James Burton, CEO, California Public Employees' Retirement System
18. King Fahd, king of Saudi Arabia
19. David Kessler, commissioner, U.S. Food and Drug Administration
20. Don Phillips, publisher, Morningstar Mutual Funds
21. Jesse Helms, senator from North Carolina; chairman, Senate Foreign Relations Committee
22. James Dugan, CEO, Swiss Bank Corporation
23. Herbert Allen, partner, Allen & Co.
24. Charles I. Clough Jr., chief investment strategist, Merrill Lynch & Co., Inc.
25. Jiang Zemin, president, People's Republic of China
26. Dennis J. Keegan, managing director, Salomon Brothers
27. Dan Hertzberg, national news editor, *Wall Street Journal*
28. E. E. "Buzz" Geduld, president, Herzog, Heine, Geduld, Inc.
29. Fred Grauer, CEO, Wells Fargo Nikko Investment Advisors
30. Richard G. Sherlund, partner, Goldman, Sachs & Co.
31. Abby Cohen, cochair of the Investment Policy Committee, Goldman, Sachs & Co.
32. Dan Dorfman, market writer and commentator
33. Charles Schwab, chairman, Charles Schwab & Co, Inc.
34. Boris Yeltsin, president, Russia
35. Edward Hyman Jr., chairman of the International Strategy and Investment Group
36. William Gross, managing director, PIMCO Advisors, L.P.
37. C. Fred Bergsten, director, Institute for International Economics
38. Leon Black, founder, Apollo Advisors, L.P.
39. Anne Bingaman, assistant attorney general, Antitrust Division

40. Neil Perry, head of Latin American Research, Baring Securities
41. Alan Blinder, vice chairman, Federal Reserve Board
42. William T. Allen, chancellor, Court of Chancery of Delaware
43. Richard Scott, president and CEO, Columbia/HCA Healthcare Corporation
44. Paul Tudor Jones, chairman, Tudor Investment Corp.
45. Tomiichi Murayama, prime minister, Japan
46. Martin Zweig, newsletter publisher and investor
47. Leo O'Neill, chief ratings officer, Standard & Poor's
48. Rupert Murdoch, chairman and CEO, NewsCorp, Ltd.
49. Maryann Keller, managing director and automotive analyst, Furman Seiz, Inc.
50. Saddam Hussein, president, Iraq

Chapter 6   A Manufacturing CEO

Susan J. Ganz

> Few ideas are in themselves practical. It is for want of imagination in
> applying them, rather than in acquiring them, that they fail. The
> creative process does not end with an idea—it only starts with an
> idea.

> John Arnold (MIT, 1956)
> *Business Week*, December 29, 1956

You might call Susan Ganz a master translator. When the
30-something Wharton MBA graduate in finance and multinational
management became the chief executive officer of Lion Brothers, Inc. in
1989, the venerable manufacturer of embroidered products was in trouble.
The Baltimore-based company, which dominated the industry for close to
one hundred years, had lost market share to competitors with cheaper
labor and structural costs in other countries; the equipment was
antiquated, and the staff was poorly managed.

"We now have about 20 percent of the entire emblem market," says
Ganz proudly, naming companies, organizations, and individuals whose
uniforms wear the Lion Brothers' patches—the National Football League,
the National Hockey League, Coca-Cola, Nike, the Boy Scouts and Girl
Scouts of America, and superstars Michael Jordan and Wayne Gretsky
among them.

Embroidered patches line the walls of the Lion Brothers' office.
There you will see the official seals for the Army, Navy, and yes, the
president of the United States.

It is in the emblem "collectibles" market that Lion Brothers has developed a healthy share in the past few years. The company adds historical significance and interest to past sporting events by packaging embroidered emblems in its "Limited Editions" line, commemorating events for the National Football League, the National Hockey League, and the National Association for Stock Car Racing. It also provides commemorative emblems in the entertainment field for movies such as "Star Wars" and for numerous Disney movies and other events. There is also a strong demand for Civil War memorabilia, and Lion meets it by making emblems of flags.

"In addition," says Ganz, "old patterns and designs that we developed over the past hundred years are now being reissued as Limited Edition collectibles. The objective of our collectible package is not for it to be worn, but for it to be enjoyed."

Most recently, Lion Brothers, which employs close to 1,000 people worldwide in a variety of positions from loom technicians and product finishers to executive management, has doubled its revenues since 1994 in the headwear division. It has extended the manufacturing of hats to designing labels that go on them for the Boy Scouts, the National Park Service, the rapidly growing alumni markets in colleges and universities, and for Donna Karan fashion shows.

Looking for Ideas

How does CEO Susan Ganz find out about the ever-changing emblem market? Probably the most underrated resource a business can have, Ganz believes, is ideas. And the best way to come up with ideas is to read. "I'm an information junkie," she claims with a smile. "I read everything...there's nothing better for me than a day at the bookstore or online."

For inspiration and advice, Ganz looks to many of the traditional periodicals that business people turn to. "The basics for me are the *New York Times*, the *Wall Street Journal*, *Forbes*, *Fortune*, and *Business Week*," she says.

For information on the embroidered product manufacturers and markets, she reads *Apparel Strategist* and *Stitches*. Also on her reading list are numerous licensing and consumer trend publications such as *Team Licensing Letter*, *Sports Style*, and *Sports Collectors Digest*.

Susan Ganz says that many of her best business ideas come from a range of general interest publications, such as *People* magazine, *In Style*, *Cosmopolitan*, *New York,* and *The New Yorker.* "I don't separate my reading into business and leisure," she notes. "*People* magazine may have some sort of bearing on my business. In *In Style*, you see what people are wearing, what shows are popular, what movies are coming out."

The grocery store magazine *People* has been the source for several big merchandising connections Lion Brothers has nabbed: Star Wars collectibles, Disney products, and the car racing association.

"To some extent, in the soft goods industry, you're always looking for the next style," says Ganz, explaining her need to constantly come up with new ideas and new markets for Lion Brothers products. "You're never stuck at point zero. The business is always dynamic, it never stops."

Ganz says that there are numerous other ways to scan the environment for good ideas. Staff provide important information, as do vendors, customers, friends, and developments in other geographical environments.

Translating Information into Ideas

Recognizing a good opportunity is only half the battle, however. The second component of Ganz's and Lion Brothers' success is found in the company's aggressive methods of utilizing these ideas and translating them into work, that is, interrelating the needs.

Rather than sending out solicitations for business and waiting for responses, Lion Brothers often works in tandem with clients to create their products. Ganz doesn't believe in just banging the product out quickly and taking the fee. "Lion Brothers develops long-standing relationships with customers, and customers really respect the support we offer them," says Ganz. "We work best when we work in partnerships with organizations in determining and articulating what it is they really want and need."

Often this kind of relationship requires Lion Brothers to take the initiative in suggesting designs for embroidered patches to their clients. Ganz uses Wayne Gretzky's record-breaking 802nd goal commemorative patch as an example: "In sporting goods, one of the trends is collectibles," says Ganz. "So we may say to a licensee of the National Hockey League, 'Wayne Gretzky's about to get his 802nd goal, and this is a very big event.' If we make a thousand patches for the event and he signs them, the jerseys that are worth $100 on the market become $1,000 items because of our patch and his signature."

Lion Brothers can approach companies in this fashion because of its reputation as a high-quality, as well as a value-added manufacturer. "As a value-added producer, we provide the idea to the customer. Therefore the customer is generally willing to pay more. A client would typically ask a commodity producer, 'How fast can we do it and how much will it cost?' But it's a different thing we're offering." In fact, she points out that Lion Brothers is not considered a commodity supplier; it now offers services (i.e., customized work) to complement its products..."and that's where we can and do truly differentiate ourselves."

The Analysis

Once a popular trend has been identified, the creative team at Lion Brothers quickly goes to work to analyze how the company can make it into a product. "It's something like a decision tree," Ganz says. "First we decide what the objective is, and then we work backwards and say, 'Who do we contact in order to get to there?' Our sales and marketing department may perform market research. We'll also call up the heads of licensing at some other places. Or we may go to the leagues directly. We will also use resources, such as *Team Licensing Letter*, trade shows, or contacts in other companies who may have suggestions, recommendations, or leads."

For example, behind the company's push to design patches for the NFL is a certain mindset. As she notes: "We say, are there licensees involved? If not, perhaps we should work with one of our customers to become one [a licensee]. If there are, let's find out who they are."

Translating Cultures

Lion Brothers has an added built-in challenge that makes translation of another kind of the highest importance: Half of the company's employees work in a manufacturing plant in the People's Republic of China.

When dealing with a country as removed from the American business world as China, Ganz says, the traditional sources of information just don't work. "By the time *The Economist* or the *Wall Street Journal* sends a reporter over there to cover local events, something has already happened. They're reporting on past events. By the time events appear on the online services, the information is dated."

Ganz believes that relationships are currently built through vendors and customers. Especially when dealing with the Chinese, one has to utilize what she calls "the basic form of information—interpersonal relationships."

> To understand what's going on in China, one has to understand the culture, the language, and the history, and one has to talk to the people. I hire people who are multicultural and have a variety of language skills. They have to understand the Western culture and to be able to translate what they're thinking in an Eastern way into something a Westerner can understand. For example, if there is an important holiday for the people, we can't, as Americans, just decide to work on that day and give them another day off. There are serious cultural issues which must be taken into consideration.

Ganz notes that she also has her own office staffed with people from all over the world. As a result, her associates are fluent in various cultures and can talk whatever cultural language is required to facilitate direct communication.

In addition to communicating with a Chinese audience, Lion Brothers has begun to explore relationships with other manufacturers in Taiwan, Indonesia, Malaysia, "and other countries that simply don't do business the same way Americans do," Ganz says. Of course, expanding into foreign markets will only expand the difficulty and the importance of gathering information.

From Screens to Stitches

But Chinese isn't the only language that the Lion Brothers staff need to know. Today there's an entirely new language and culture whose applications are just beginning to be discovered: the language of the computer.

Investments made in factory computer technology are already paying off in her business. "The looms are now computer controlled, whereas they used to be rolled off of a jacquard roll that resembles that of a piano player," she says. "Now, whenever there's a mistake in the machine, the operator can simply go to the computer, click a few buttons, and change a single stitch out of thousands." To the outsider, factory-stitched embroidery might not seem like an industry likely to be on the cutting edge of computer technology. Not so, claims Ganz, who has been bringing concepts to Lion Brothers that have until recently been the province of the high-tech community.

High-Tech Ideas: Transmitting Information and Electronic ID Codes

What other high-tech ideas are in the works at Lion Brothers? Ganz answers:

Radio frequency ID codes (RFID) embedded inside patches for security purposes. We asked, "What do emblems do?" They identify a place or an event or an organization. We said, "Wouldn't it be interesting if a patch could identify the person it's attached to?" Instead of just being something that's visual, maybe it could transmit data about the person who's wearing it. We want to put it inside the emblem. The challenge is to make it cost-effective and launderable and we are working on that.

Organizing the Information Flow of a CEO

One of the keys to ultimately implementing new ideas is for a CEO to manage many forms of information in order to survive the information deluge. Susan Ganz is working on ways to organize the morass of paper that usually fills her desk: "When I file something, the chance of bringing it back is around five percent," she says. "The goal is to organize information in categories that fit one's own needs or to create subject specialties that relate to how one processes information. It is more efficient that way, and you can get to things in a more directed fashion."

"I've come up with a new test," she says. "I carry something for three to six months, and if I don't look it up during that time, I just take the whole thing and throw it out, because if I haven't missed it by then, chances are I won't miss it. It's a survival technique in the information age."

Going Beyond Traditional Thinking

The concepts that brought Lion Brothers back to the top of the market aren't so revolutionary, Ganz claims. They just require knowing how to think and to translate ideas in today's changing information environment. "There is a limited pool of people who can adapt to the computer age," she notes. "There's a tremendous opportunity out there, but one needs to go beyond traditional thinking."

That's not to say that today's successful business person needs to be a tech wizard. Ganz approves of the holistic approach to business, the approach where you need to mesh the big picture with the day-to-day structure:

> I'm a generalist. My best people are people who are generalists but who come with specific functional skills. Everyone brings a piece to something else...This cross-functional organization needs to be linked, to be able to obtain, retrieve, and send. But they also need to connect, i.e., to understand. Sales has to connect with manufacturing, manufacturing has to connect with pre-process, pre-process has to connect with finance. It's really all about creating a network of colleagues that work in a cooperative fashion, and the personal network is the key because it goes beyond transmitting information. It takes it to a new place—one of understanding.

With the emergence of the Internet, there are many new opportunities for Lion Brothers, and it is already beginning to prove valuable for translating pattern designs and for the potential of developing electronic brochures, says Ganz. "Because patterns [in the brochures] change so rapidly, the cost of printing each one every time you do a catalog is enormous. Changing that pattern electronically would reduce the cost significantly."

Currently, a companywide intranet for communicating and connecting is under development. "We are just beginning to see the enormous potential for direct communication as a means to establish relationships with customers or as a link to subcontractors in far-off places," Ganz says. For example, she thinks that providing a subcontractor in Indonesia with a laptop computer that has a telecommunications protocol already programmed in it will make it easy for them to track orders with Lion Brothers or to communicate information in ways not possible before the Internet. She also talks about putting some educational support tools on the company Web page, such as an online tutorial, that will allow contractors to learn more about Lion Brothers and the process of making emblems.

"The potential is there for our Web page to be a terrific tool," says Ganz. "It decreases the cost of distribution dramatically. The ability to go up on the Internet and check production information between our manufacturing locations with just a local call will dramatically reduce our costs."

"Using this method of communication eliminates the necessity of sending somebody over to Indonesia next week," she explains. "So, it's not that we don't visit the customers because, again, so much of it is personal relationships, but the timing of the visit becomes one of choice for the customer and the vendor instead of one of necessity."

Chapter 7   A Public Relations Executive

Phyllis Brotman

"When your circus comes to town and you put up a sign, that's advertising.
If you put the sign on the back of an elephant and you march the elephant through town, that's sales promotion.
If the elephant, with the sign still on his back, tramples through the mayor's flower garden and the paper reports it, that's publicity.
If you can get the mayor to laugh about it and forgive the elephant and ride in the circus with no hard feelings, then you've mastered the art of public relations."

Raleigh Pinskey, *The Zen of Hype,*
An Insider's Guide to the Publicity Game, 1991

"You have to learn the client's business—that's the first thing you do after you learn that you have gotten the account. You can't write for a client and do events for them if you don't know what they are all about," says Phyllis Brotman. "We find out about our clients' (or their competitors') business in various ways: We conduct an Internet search, we also get companies' materials, and we learn what their mission statement is."

Phyllis Brotman has mastered the art of public relations (PR), and her mastery is evidenced by the numerous plaques, awards, and honors that were bestowed on her by professional associations and are hanging on the walls of Image Dynamics' corporate office. Awards such as The Silver Anvil from the Public Relations Society of America and the Clio from the American Association of Advertising Agencies reflect more than 30 years of hard work in the field.

Launched in 1966, Image Dynamics, Inc. is a full-service public relations and advertising agency that has been honored locally as "Baltimore's Best Small Company" since 1988 by *Baltimore Magazine.* In 1994, Brotman was named one of "Maryland's 50 Most Powerful People" by The *Baltimore Business Journal,* and in 1996, "Maryland's Top 100 Women" by *Warfield's Business Magazine.*

Developing Her Own Knowledge Bases: "Been There, Done That" Experiences

In her early career, Phyllis Brotman worked for a television station where she was given the opportunity to work in every department when others were away from the office, and so she learned about filmmaking, film editing, film scheduling, and public relations. Brotman recollects even earlier times:

> I really think I started in public relations when I was around seven or eight years old, because I was very active in my elementary school selling savings stamps during World War II—I would come up with all kinds of events to raise money for savings stamps and bonds, but I didn't know it was public relations. All through elementary and junior high school, I was active in many community organizations that gave me the confidence that I now have to be in business.

Brotman says that throughout her childhood, her supportive, forward-thinking parents helped channel her energies for her future role as mediator and counselor to clients, which now include health care companies and hospitals, hotels, tourist attractions, the media, law firms, insurance companies, manufacturers, sports teams, developers, retail businesses, and financial institutions.

The staff of 22 at Image Dynamics includes Brotman's daughter, now president of the company, and a number of account executives in media and public relations, media buyers, copywriters, artists and graphic designers, and researchers.

The services provided by Image Dynamics are typical of most public relations firms:

Public Relations—press relations, special events, meetings, conventions and seminars, community relations, personal appearances and speaking engagements, government liaison, crisis planning, and internal communications.

Advertising—media planning and buying; copywriting; print, audio and video production; marketing research and analysis; ad placement; and ad tracking.

Marketing Communications—primary research, secondary research, communications strategy, advertising and collateral materials, and coordination of services.

Graphic Design—brochures, information kits, annual reports, newsletters, catalogues, posters, direct mail, recruitment, reports/proposals.

Brotman notes that Image Dynamics goes outside for in-depth research, photography, printing, and TV and radio production, because they don't have those facilities on site. But all of the other services are available in-house.

She cites concrete examples of the kinds of services provided to clients:

- When the then governor of Maryland, William Donald Schaefer, needed an international voice to promote trade missions abroad, Image Dynamics made the news of the missions available to decision makers worldwide through the Voice of America, Radio Free Europe, ABC News, AP, UPI, *Business Week*, and other local, national, and international media outlets.

- When a local power tool company wanted to introduce a new consumer product, Image Dynamics convinced "a record 51 million people" to take a close look at it and also provided press coverage, beefed up trade shows, and renewed consumer interest for the entire line of power tools.

- When a national HMO entered the market, Image Dynamics wrote the program for immediate name recognition with an award-winning total communications program through advertising, public relations, and meeting planning.

Defining Public Relations:
Spin Is Everything

What is public relations? If you browse through the business section of any bookstore these days, you are likely to see titles such as *Sports Publicity, CEO Credibility, Image Wars, Tainted Truth, Crisis Management, Selling Your Story to Wall Street, Lobbying for Your Cause, Planned Events, Selling God,* and *The Age of Propaganda* that are all written by public relations experts or consultants who provide insight into how companies, institutions, individuals, or issues can become more valued, understood, or protected. Public relations is an art that reflects mastery of spin and image, "hype," i.e., perceptions and truth.

Or perhaps you are familiar with the annual issue of *Fortune* that features the top ten of America's Most Admired Corporations. Here corporate reputations are judged by industry experts on eight attributes: quality of management; quality of products or services; innovativeness; long-term investment value; financial soundness; ability to attract, develop, and keep talented people; responsibility to the community and the environment; and wise use of corporate assets. (Note: *Fortune* also lists the bottom ten.) The winners are strategists not only in their own businesses, but in broadcasting their success to the world, a major component of PR.

Brotman explains her own definition of public relations:

> Public relations is a nominal way to reach the target audiences that we want to pursue. If we are doing consumer product publicity, we would reach the publications that product is good for. For example, with power tools, we would reach the home mechanics and the do-it-yourself magazines. If we are doing something with the lawn mower, we would reach lawn and garden publications. If we were working with health care, we would reach the medical and consumer publications. So we can target our audience pretty well with public relations.

The Public Relations Society of America (PRSA),[1] located in New York and considered the leading professional society for public relations practitioners, provides a more formal definition of public relations: "Public relations helps an organization and its publics adapt mutually to each other."[2] The society says that in this definition, the essential functions of research, planning, communications dialogue, and evaluation are implied.

Brotman continues:

> Public relations can be fun, but there's a great deal of responsibility at your end, because your clients are spending their money with you, and you need to make sure that their money is spent properly. If you are working with the public, there is a responsibility there, because you are putting out some sort of message...and there has to be integrity in your message, because you are representing a company or organization.

The Benefits of Public Relations

The society also describes other ways in which public relations efforts help management and benefit society[3]:

For management: Public relations paves the way for sale of products or services, builds morale, enhances productivity, provides early warning systems, provides an organization with new opportunities, helps protect an organization under attack, helps organizations manage change, and helps maintain an organization's relationship to its social responsibility.

For society: Public relations speaks for the public to organizations and speaks to organizations for the public; it can activate social conscience and enhance communications between diverse groups.

The PRSA: Multifaceted Knowledge Bases with Extensive Information Needs

The *Public Relations Professional Career Guide*[4] says that within the PRSA's 15,000 membership (estimated to be 10 percent of all public relations practitioners), there are 108 chapters, 10 geographic districts, and 16 professional interest groups that provide specialized public relations services and information to their clients. Each group has a newsletter containing articles on the specialized knowledge/information needs, skills, and strategies to perform the functions that are distinct to that group. The spectrum of groups the society serves includes associations, corporations, counselors, academies, educational and cultural organizations, educators, employee communications, environments, financial communications, food and beverage, the International Health Academy, professional services, public affairs and government, social services, technology, and travel and tourism.

The "publics" (clients) served by these professional interest groups are also defined in *Public Relations: An Overview.*[5]

- Employee (e.g., management, union members, retirees)
- Community (e.g., neighborhood coalitions, community organizations, plant locations, Chambers of Commerce)
- Customer (geographical by location) or functional (by job)
- Industry/business (e.g., suppliers, competitors, professional societies, trade associations)
- Media (e.g., general, foreign, trade, specialized)
- Academia (e.g., trustees, regents, administration, and alumni)
- Investment/financial (e.g., analysts, institutional holders, shareholders, portfolio managers, bankers)
- Governmental (e.g., geographical and functional—legislative, regulatory, executive, judicial)
- Special interest (e.g., environmental, safety, handicapped, minority, think tanks, consumer, health, religious)

PR's Specialized Information Needs: Learning to Ask "What" and Also "Why"

The PRSA Foundation, a part of the society, fosters research and education for public relations[6] and gives examples of the specialized knowledge and skills that might be required in the professional practice of public relations and communications:

> Communication arts, psychology, social psychology, sociology, political science, economics, and the principles of management and ethics. Technical knowledge and skills are required for opinion research, public issues analysis, media relations, direct mail, institutional advertising, publications, film/video productions, special events, speeches, and presentations.

PR agencies must access and utilize information of many different kinds to accomplish their goals. It is not just a matter of getting the word out to the organizations or individuals or groups; it is also finding out what people are thinking and getting the word back to the organization. While much of the information sought for clients is quantifiable data, such as how many people intend to vote for a candidate or buy a product, often the search extends into broader, qualitative measures, such as discovering why people think and feel the way they do, or how to change attitudes and behaviors. One-on one interviews, focus groups, and tracking studies are ways to accomplish these goals. Formulating strategies, sizing up the competition, swaying opinion, and getting publicity are examples of outcomes of the practice.

PR Case Studies

Case studies in public relations that demonstrate excellence in the methodologies of research, planning, execution, and evaluation can be found by looking at PRSA's Silver Anvil Awards, housed in the PRSA information center in New York. Examples of Anvil winners include: "Aerosol Industry Battles CFC Misinformation" (Ketchum Public Relations, for the Consumer Aerosol Products Council); "History in the Making" (Duffey Communications, for the Georgia Lottery Corporation); and "Tall Ship Rose: Recycled Plastics Sail the Potomac" (Fleishmann-Hillard, Inc., for the American Plastics Council).

In 1992, Image Dynamics was a Silver Anvil winner for the Black & Decker Company's 75th anniversary. Brotman describes the project:

> Black & Decker, the worldwide leader in the power tools industry, has built its multibillion dollar success on the power drill, a market the company still dominates. In 1992, their introduction of the first keyless chuck coincided with the 75th anniversary of the pistol-grip, trigger switch drill—the tool that launched the company. This anniversary presented an unprecedented opportunity to capitalize on the company's heritage of product innovation.

Brotman explains that the public relations program developed by Image Dynamics included a media tour, newspaper mailings, video news releases, and special ceremonies at Black & Decker's manufacturing plant, the Smithsonian Institution, and the 1992 National Hardware Show, "all designed to garner maximum publicity and awareness."

And the result was:

> The campaign was successful in achieving its goals—increasing sales of electric drills and revitalizing a stagnant market for do-it-yourself electric drills. Black & Decker directly credits the 75th anniversary public relations campaign with boosting sales of power drills by a remarkable 22 percent, which roughly translates into a $10 million sales increase.

The Press Release

Press releases are the mainstay of PR, and they are carried by many news wire services and online databases and now the Internet. Companies, organizations, and people issue press releases chiefly to maintain a high public profile. For example, a press release might promote the launch of a new product or announce increased revenues, stock splits, or dividends. Or it might announce the appointment of a new chief executive officer or the installation of new members of a board of directors. It reflects a company's image.

Below is an example of a press release, compiled by Image Dynamics and found on the PR Newswire database through DIALOG® Information Services File 613:

DIALOG® File 613:PR Newswire
©1995 PR Newswire Association Inc. All rts. reserv.
BALTIMORE-BASED DEWALT SHIPS $50,000 IN POWER TOOLS TO HURRICANE RAVAGED AREAS
Date: August 27, 1992   20:11 EDT
Word Count: 217
What: The DeWALT® Industrial Tool Co. is sending out a new shipment of loaner tools to Hurricane Andrew-ravaged Dade County, Florida and Southern Louisiana, to be used for emergency repairs by home and business owners.
When: Friday, August 28
             2 p.m.
Where: Black & Decker Distribution Center
             626 Hanover Pike
             Hampstead, Maryland
             Due to the damage caused by Hurricane Andrew in Southern Louisiana and Dade County, Florida,

DeWALT® has made available more than $50,000 worth of corded and cordless high-performance power tools and a limited number of generators to power them on an emergency loaner basis.

DeWALT began shipping the tools to the hurricane-affected areas on Tuesday, Aug. 25. In addition to providing loaner tools, six DeWALT tool vans (three in each state) are providing tool drop-off and assistance with repairs.

Those in need of loaner tools can call the DeWALT toll-free hotline at 1-800-4-DEWALT (1-800-433-9258). Operators are staffing the hotline from 8 a.m. to 10 p.m. (EDT) weekdays.

The tools being provided include: circular saws, cordless drills, battery chargers and reciprocating saws. In addition, the DeWALT tool vans are providing generators.

Contact: Carolyn Brown of Image Dynamics, Inc., work 410-576-9334, or home 410-243-2746, for DeWALT Industrial Tool Co.

(Permission to reprint granted by DIALOG® and PR Newswire.)

The outcome of this press release is described by Brotman: "This was a very successful public service project that helped thousands of people affected by the hurricanes. They had the opportunity to rebuild their homes or just keep their homes running after the storms hit."

What Image Dynamics Does to Stay Informed

Image Dynamics accesses much of its information for its clients through electronic sources, such as LEXIS-NEXIS, Prodigy, and CompuServe, which has a public relations forum. Use of the Internet's specialized resources is growing at this time for doing research and for seeing what other companies can offer.

In addition, membership in the Public Relations Society of America and the American Society of Advertising Agencies allows Image

Dynamics to tap the organizations' libraries for reprints of current and historical articles for a fee.

Brotman explains how she thinks about research:

> By doing research, we have the opportunity to show the client why we should be doing the work. It supports the work we do. If there are areas that are not clear to the consumer, we can do a campaign that will verify that information based on research. We use research in decision making and in management. An interesting way we do our research is through Advertising and Marketing International Network (AMIN), a network of public relations, advertising, and marketing agencies around the world. When we are preparing materials for a presentation, we might call our AMIN partners, if they have an account such as the one we are researching, and ask them what interesting ideas they use. Then, we discuss those suggestions and may choose to include them in our work.

As Phyllis Brotman reviews her work over the past 30 years and looks forward to the future, she comments on the changes that are occurring in public relations:

> Public relations will be getting more complex. There are many more media to deal with, and there are many more areas than we can conceive on computer networks...target markets are tremendously diverse, and it will change the way we do public relations. Computers are coming down in price, so everyone will have a computer like a TV. It will be required for life to do your banking, shopping, and all the things that are done now during a day's work. I think the work will come to that. I think issues in public relations get more complicated, because when you reach a reporter, you get either the e-mail or you do it on the network...and you never get to talk with them. It's a very intensive business and very difficult on the psyche, with emotional highs and lows, but on the other hand, it has its moments, and we share in the glory and awards that come our way.

Notes

1.   *Public Relations: An Overview,* Monograph Series (New York: The PRSA Foundation, 1991).
2.   Ibid, 2.
3.   Ibid, 9.

4.   *Public Relations Professional Career Guide* (New York: The PRSA Foundation, 1993), 60.
5.   *Public Relations: An Overview,* Monograph Series (New York: The PRSA Foundation, 1991).
6.   Ibid, 5.

For More Information

I   Public relations electronic sites:

- Public Relations Society of America (PRSA): http://www. prsa.org
- American Association of Advertising Agencies (AAAA): http://www.commercepark.com/AAAA
- International Association of Business Communicators: http://www.iabc.com/
- PR Newswire: http//www.PRNewswire.com
- CompuServe (public relations forum): http://www.Compuserv. com

II.   Public relations periodicals and newsletters:

Jack O'Dwyer's *PR Newsletter,* 271 Madison Avenue, New York, NY 10016 (212-679-2471)
PR Reporter, Box 600, Dudley House, Exeter, NH 03833 (603-778-0514)
Public Relations News, 1201 Seven Locks Road, Potomac, MD 20854-3394 (301-340-1520)
Public Relations Quarterly, 44 W. Market St., POB 311, Rhinebeck, NY 12572 (914-876-2081)
Public Relations Review, Jai Press, 55 Old Post Rd. #2, Greenwich, CT 06836-6200 (203-661-7602)
Ragan Report, 212 West Superior St., #200, Chicago, IL 60605 (312-922-8245)

III. Other public relations publications:

The Public Relations Society of America (212-995-0757) publishes two monthly newspapers for public relations practitioners: *Public Relations Tactics* (http://www.prsa.org/tactics.html) features news information and how-to advice provided by practitioners, and the *Public Reactions Strategist* (http://www.prsa.org/strat.html) provides a forum for discussion and commentary on issues facing senior practitioners and the companies and clients they serve. It incorporates viewpoints from CEOs, social scientists, psychologists, top government officials, and researchers, and the emphasis is on long-term strategy and planning policies.

Two books, *The Unseen Power: Public Relations, A History* and *Public Relations History from the 17th to the 20th Century* (Hillsdale, NJ: Lawrence Erlbaum Associates, 1995), both by Scott M. Cutlip, dean emeritus, the University of Georgia, and the field's long-time leading scholar, historian, and teacher, provide an inside view of the way public relations has developed and been practiced over time. He says:

> Public relations or its equivalents—propaganda, publicity, public information—began when mankind started to live together in tribal camps where one's survival depended upon others. To function, civilization requires communication, conciliation, consensus, and cooperation—the bedrock fundamental of the public relations function. For example, the book describes the 17th century efforts of land promoters and colonists to lure settlers from Europe—mainly England—to a primitive land along the Atlantic coast. They used publicity, tracts, sermons, and letters to disseminate rosy, glowing accounts of life and opportunity in the new land.

Part 2   Information Professionals and Practitioners

Profiles

Information professionals, as practitioners of information retrieval and usage in business or corporate environments, generally service the end users within the organization. They are not usually the top decision makers, but their research can affect the corporate or institutional decision-making process in important strategic ways. Because of their intimate knowledge of the information environment (information professionals make a living identifying, gathering, and using information), they generally know the company's strategic plan, corporate structure, and important issues that impact its growth. They also know outside information resources (print and electronic) that are subject-specific to companies' or clients' information needs, and they can evaluate the content provided by creators and vendors of information resources. In addition, they have a strong network of other information professionals, frequently sharing subject specialties, new resources, and techniques. Those who are designated as information professionals are generally educated in the information sciences or hold a Master's of Library Science (MLS) degree from a program accredited by the American Library Association (ALA) institution.

The role of information professionals and practitioners is rapidly evolving, particularly in business. Constituencies or clients increasingly refer to them as guides, pathfinders, trailblazers, knowbots, cybrarians, knowledge agents, and counselors in the information retrieval process. For some clients, information professionals are providing "customized and/or analyzed" information.

Information professionals and practitioners interviewed include:

Marjorie L. Hill, Director, The Ben Franklin Business Information Center, Philadelphia, Pennsylvania

Director of an economic development information center, Marjorie Hill tells how in 1990 a market study conducted by an economic development organization in Pennsylvania revealed that 80 percent of small businesses did not use online searching of any kind and that 18 percent used it very little. As a result of this study, she was hired to help establish a program to provide electronic information demonstrating the value of information to the business and technology community, and it became one of the most highly respected economic development programs in the country.

Daan Boom, Manager, Informatie & Research Centrum, KPMG, Amsterdam, Netherlands

Manager of an information center in a "Big Six" multinational consulting firm, Daan Boom describes how his professional staff has become more proactive in meeting the information needs of accountants and consultants, not only in the local office but globally, and how partnering with functional teams for strategic planning support has added new efficiencies to the company and strengthened the value and image of the information professional throughout the corporation.

Denise Cumming, Founding Partner, Connect Research, Minneapolis, Minnesota

A former "knowledge analyst" at Teltech in Minneapolis, Denise Cumming discusses her matter-of-fact views about the value of hiring an experienced information searcher for highly specialized electronic research. She provides examples of database nuances and why it is important to know about them when doing sophisticated research. She also discusses why she thinks human intelligence is better for information gathering than is artificial intelligence.

Sue Rugge, President, The Information Professionals Institute, Oakland, California

Information brokering has been reported in the press as one of the hottest entrepreneurial opportunities of the Information Age. Sue Rugge has been a trailblazer in defining this business niche and is regarded by her colleagues as "the mother of the information brokering industry." Rugge has been an information service provider, but more recently serves as a teacher/mentor to aspiring information brokers and as an advisor to the information community.

Allan E. Rypka, Vice President, Research, Focused Research International, Leonardtown, Maryland

Director of research for his own company, Allan Rypka specializes in law enforcement, intelligence, and information technology. He explains how his education in military intelligence and his experiences in communication and navigation systems have enabled him to work in the rapidly emerging field of information warfare.

Guy St. Clair, President, InfoManage/SMR International, New York City

A provider of library and knowledge management services, Guy St. Clair's professional career has been dedicated to working with academic and corporate librarians in some of the world's finest collections of knowledge. Now a consultant, author, and publisher to the library/information services profession, St. Clair discusses the important need for companies large and small to have an information policy, and he explains the importance of conducting an information audit to identify users' information needs and to help determine the focus of the information policy.

For More Information

In 1996, the Special Libraries Association issued a report summarizing the professional and personal competencies that will be required of its members in light of the rapid social, technological, and workplace transformations that are taking place. *Competencies for Special Librarians of the 21st Century* edited by Barbara M. Spiegelman

(Washington, DC: Special Libraries Association, 1997), is useful as a standard for defining required skills of all future knowledge workers. These competencies are:

Professional Competencies: *The Special Librarian...*

- Has expert knowledge of the content of information resources, including the ability to critically evaluate and filter them;
- Has specialized subject knowledge appropriate to the business of the organization or client;
- Develops and manages convenient, accessible, and cost-effective information services that are aligned with the strategic directions of the organization;
- Provides excellent instruction and support for library and information service users;
- Assesses information needs and designs and markets value-added information services and products to meet identified needs;
- Uses appropriate information technology to acquire, organize, and disseminate information;
- Uses appropriate business and management approaches to communicate the importance of information services to senior management;
- Develops specialized information products for use inside or outside the organization or by individual clients;
- Evaluates the outcomes of information use and conducts research related to the solution of information management problems;
- Continually improves information services in response to changing needs;
- Is an effective member of the senior management team and a consultant to the organization on information issues.

Personal Competencies: *The Special Librarian...*

- is committed to service excellence;
- seeks out challenges and sees new opportunities both inside and outside the library;
- sees the big picture;
- looks for partnerships and alliances;

- creates an environment of mutual respect and trust;
- has effective communication skills;
- works well with others in a team;
- provides leadership;
- plans, prioritizes, and focuses on what is critical;
- is committed to life-long learning and personal career planning;
- has personal business skills and creates new opportunities;
- recognizes the value of professional networking and solidarity;
- is flexible and positive in a time of continuing change.

Another Special Libraries Association publication, edited by Hope N. Tillman of Babson College, is called *Internet Tools of the Profession: A Guide for Information Professionals*, second edition (Washington, Special Libraries Association, 1997). The book provides specialized Internet resources recommended by and for business and academic librarians relating to such areas as business and finance, information technology, education, food, agriculture and nutrition, information technology, insurance and employee benefits, legal, pharmaceutical telecommunications, and more.

Chapter 8   A Director of an Economic Development Information Center

Marjorie L. Hill

> ...the function of entrepreneurs is to reform or revolutionize the pattern of production by exploiting an invention or more generally, an untried technological possibility for producing a new way by opening up a new source of supply of materials or a new outlet for products...

> Joseph A. Schumpeter,
> *Capitalism, Socialism, and Democracy,* 1942

On Market Street in Philadelphia, surrounded by two of Pennsylvania's largest universities, the University of Pennsylvania and Drexel, sits the Ben Franklin Technology Center of Southeastern Pennsylvania (BFTC), an economic development organization of the state of Pennsylvania and the largest source of seed capital for technology development in the region. Within BFTC is the Business Information Center (BIC), supplier of an equally critical resource for the economic development of the region: electronic information.

Marjorie Hill—Implementing a
New Industry Category

Although all of the Ben Franklin Partnership programs have been successful, it is the Business Information Center in the BFTC in Philadelphia that has received the most attention in recent years. (Author's note: See For More Information, III for overall results of the Ben Franklin Partnership Program.) To learn about the evolution and development of its information services, you would talk to Marjorie Hill, developer and director of the Center and one of the pioneers of the information industry who has helped business and technology companies gain a better understanding of the strategic uses of information.

Electronic Information:
A Key Economic Development
Tool for the 21st Century

Hill explains that state and federal funds from resources such as the U.S. Small Business Administration, the National Institute for Standards and Technology, and a collaboration with Pennsylvania's Small Business Development Centers were allocated for the Business Information Center (BIC) following a 1990 market research study conducted by the Ben Franklin Technology Center revealing that 80 percent of small businesses and new technology companies do not use online searching of any kind, and the remaining 18 percent have used it very little. The assumption was that if businesses don't start using information, they cannot compete within their industry or with international companies. As a result of the study, a program was funded and initiated to provide access to business and technical information already available in electronic format. Essentially, the program would jump-start a new industry category of the information age: electronic information retrieval services.

The initial goal of the BIC was to improve business decision making by providing market, industry, and competitive information that is normally too difficult or costly for small and emerging technology companies to acquire on their own.

Key clients for BIC's services were to come from the small business sector that leads economic revival in many communities. Fledgling businesses would be encouraged and permitted to access electronic database information on a low-cost basis subsidized by the state.

Other BIC clients would come from 16 public access points located within the state's Small Business Development Centers (SBDCs), where small businesses come for assistance in developing business and marketing plans. Once the BIC was established, a program was funded that allowed its staff members to teach research skills and provide research assistance to SBDC staff members who could then work independently with their own clients. This BIC program also included presentations to SBDC clients and consulting for complex research projects.

Information Literacy Training
for Businesses

Now that the BIC is well established, its services have evolved to meet the specialized information needs of its business and technology clients by providing:

- Seminars designed to provide information about the resources in public databases, how to access the information, and how to improve the retrieval process that include:
  - Effective business research
  - Information audits
  - Helping clients address their information needs
  - Market research on the Internet
  - Developing new products, entering new markets
  - Internet basics
- Consulting services to help develop search strategies and identify appropriate databases.
- Technical assistance during search activities.
- Custom search design and execution.
- Computer printouts of journal articles and other electronic information.

The information now available through the Business Information Center is used by companies (clients) to:

- Assemble market research and gather competitive intelligence to devise effective marketing strategies.
- Analyze market, industry, and economic trends to develop or improve business plans.

- Identify government regulations and industry experts when planning technical processes.
- Find the sources needed to enhance business, such as distributors, potential manufacturers, venture partners, and funding resources.
- Gather relevant information for writing proposals and finding solutions to technical problems.

The Benefits

The Business Information Center's promotional literature emphasizes the benefits of using its services to fulfill a company's information needs:

- *Time and Money Saved*—Undertaking a search at a library frequently requires many hours of valuable staff time. A search completed by the center is quick and often yields information that cannot be obtained from manual searches.
- *Professional Assistance*—Information specialists at the Business Information Center are experienced in retrieving relevant information for business applications. The center's staff develops effective search strategies, identifies appropriate databases, executes online searches, and quickly delivers customized results.
- *Organized Results*—The Business Information Center provides its clients with an organized, comprehensive report that identifies pertinent articles, references, and additional sources.

Electronic Database Search Examples

"Clients' search requests are varied, from simple to complex," says Marjorie Hill. "A client might request information about a company, a particular area or department within a company, a person who has worked for a company, recent new developments within a company, or a company's position within an industry." The types of information that are most in demand are marketing information, competitive intelligence, industry trends, and patent searches, she notes. She also reports that questions on the international marketplace are increasing. On the technical side, queries are related to product/process, development/modification, patent and regulatory processes. On the nontechnical side, marketing, management planning, trade name, and vendor questions are common.

Following are examples of searches conducted by the Business Information Center:

- A manufacturer wanted to expand overseas. BIC identified newspaper articles about federal programs that help manufacturers export equipment to Central Europe.
- A midsized accounting firm was studying a new market. BIC produced a list of associations that publish industry trends and provided a list of potential customers.
- A medical publisher wanted to offer a new product line of medical software. BIC located a survey on computers in medical use conducted by the American Medical Association.
- A swimming pool manufacturer needed intelligence about a competitor's advertising strategy. BIC identified a service that tracked companies' advertisements in magazines.

(Author's Note: For More Information, II provides an example of a technical search statement with the results.)

Information Retrieval Procedures at BIC

Hill explains that the initial step at BIC is to meet with a client to determine information needs. A research plan is then formulated and documented on a standardized search form developed by the BIC staff (Table 8.1).

Table 8.1 Sample Search Form Used by Information Specialists at the Ben Franklin Business Information Center

THE TOPIC
1   State the search topic in your own words.
2A   List the major concepts of the topic using three or four key terms.
2B   List the synonyms, which might be used as alternatives to the key terms.
3   What is the purpose of your search? Industry survey, market analysis, patent search, etc.

Table 8.1 (continued)

CONTENT AND FORM OF INFORMATION
4   How far back in time do you want your search to go?
5   What journals, books, reports or other publications have you used for this topic?
6   Do you know any authors that have published on this topic?

7   Will you accept:
    A.   Materials published in languages other than English _____
            If yes, which languages?_____
    B.   Materials no earlier than_____

8   You need:
    A.   Bibliographic references only _____
    B.   Abstracts only _____
    C.   Full-text articles or documents only _____
    D.   Combination depending on cost and availability _____

9   Please add any additional comments for your information request:

The information specialist then conducts an electronic search, reviews the results, processes, prints, and organizes it into sections, and provides a cover memo that states the question, the databases searched, and the results. Often, the specialist offers advice but does not actually analyze the data or make recommendations for a company's marketing plan. The specialist might say, for example, "Since the purpose of this search is to write a marketing plan, we strongly recommend you read the retrieved information before proceeding." Even though it is not their role to give advice, all information specialists at the center can draw upon years of experience in corporate libraries and each usually has more than one subject specialty.

Searching High-Powered
Online Systems

Marjorie Hill has done electronic database searching all of her professional life. After graduating from Cornell, Hill earned her M.A. in

Library and Information Services from the University of South Florida. For 18 years, she worked at Laventhol-Horwath, an international accounting firm, where she was head of its information center directing 12 information specialists. But then, Laventhol went bankrupt in 1990. Hill explains her transition to Ben Franklin:

> I subsequently left the accounting field and came to the Ben Franklin Technology Center. I wanted to put my own spin on the program, because, as an information professional, I was used to searching electronic databases at a very complex level, using boolean command language, not a menu-driven level of searching that was limited in its power to retrieve information. If my staff were to answer the sophisticated technological and business questions our clients were asking and add value in the process, we would have to do our searches on a professional level using more sophisticated, high-powered online systems.

Hill explains the work that she and her staff were doing in the initial stages of setting up the Business Information Center's development:

> We turned on our computers at 8:30 in the morning and searched 25 different systems until 5:15. We often worked at our desks all day, including lunch, to get the work out the door.

As the program began to take off, Hill recognized the importance of educating the center's managers about the value of the information she and her information specialists were bringing to the electronic information retrieval program and described its usefulness in an analogy between the skills and training of a lawyer and the skills and training of a professional information specialist:

> One realizes that if you are an intelligent, educated person and you want to get a book on how to handle a divorce, you are certainly welcome to try it on your own. Or you can go to the next level and talk to a legal paraprofessional who might be able to make some suggestions for you. But if you really want a professionally prepared legal document, you have to go to a lawyer, an attorney at law, who has studied law and passed the bar.

Hill's own manager recognized this similarity, and ultimately told her, "It has taken me a long time to understand the value of your skills."

BIC Helps Clients Articulate Their Information Needs

As director of the Business Information Center, Marjorie Hill's role has evolved to that of information consultant and mentor to executives and scientists as she helps them solve a specific problem by finding the right information. She does not mince words when it comes to explaining her experiences with information-seeking clients:

> People are messy thinkers! And I don't care if they have a Ph.D. or two Ph.D.s! They sit down and ramble about what information they think they need and how it should be organized. It is very important for clients to know what they want before we go online, because when we go online at $100 to $200 an hour, the whole thing is going to cost between $500 and $1,000. We cannot rely on messy thinking. We have to take what they are doing and make it concrete so that they understand it. Then we take that information need and state it in one or two clear, concise concepts in order to begin structuring an online search statement. Some clients learn very fast, but the initial process of identifying information needs and relating it to a business or product is excruciating for most.
>
> The best clients, and the ones who are most efficient to work with, are very clear in their thinking when they ask questions. Often, they are the ones who have done some online searching themselves. It seems that no matter how confident people are, once they get online, their confidence has dissipated within a half hour, especially when they see a bill for $1,000 and no information. That is the best teaching method that we can possibly use.

Making a Connection with Information

After 25 years as an information professional, Hill believes that still not a lot of progress has been made in using the valuable resources available online. "I have come to the conclusion that electronic data gathering is total confusion for most clients." She relates how her early clients had a vague idea that they could "talk to computers," but they were not sure how to do it. "And now you have the Internet, and they say, 'Oh yes. I know what you do now.' And I say, 'No, it's totally different,' and then it sends them into a tailspin because they are also struggling to understand the Internet."

Typically, Hill sees clients making decisions either without information or by going through unproductive activities to get the data they need, and the electronic information retrieval process is a revolutionary approach for many of them. She believes it must be analogous to reading a book from a printer of the Gutenberg era for the first time: "It is such an extreme change in cultural and cognitive patterns of information gathering and use," she says.

Although future generations of executives and scientists will be computer literate, the current generation of CEOs Hill serves still finds it difficult to understand value-added information and the specialized technical and cognitive skills that information professionals provide. "They aren't interested in the mechanics," says Hill. And she does not try to explain the technology anymore. "People want to drive the car and aren't particularly interested in inner mechanical workings." Now Hill focuses on what a client can do with the information after it is retrieved, which is all they seem to want. "They don't have time for anything else," she says.

The $500 Search Versus the $5,000 Search

Even after Hill has explained the many differences between information sources, clients do not always understand. "They have to see it and hear it a couple of times and let it sink in," she observes. What really helps explain the process is when she demonstrates that a search conducted electronically by information specialists can cost $500 dollars while a primary consultant costs $5,000.

From her experience with clients, Hill says that what businesses typically do is spend $5,000 (and sometimes even $50,000) on a consultant before they come to the Business Information Center, when it should be the other way around. She recommends that clients first see an information specialist to obtain what they can from secondary information sources and then fill in any missing pieces with primary research. Her informal definition of primary research is "any activity where humans are collecting raw data, e.g., counting people, conducting telephone surveys, creating questionnaires. It is generally unpublished, privileged information that no one else has access to." Secondary research, on the other hand, is "information that is already collected and organized in a form that can be accessed. It is published and available in print, online, and CD-ROM." The Internet, Hill says, provides both primary and secondary information.

(Author's note: See For More Information for resources used for clients at the BIC, including comments about the Internet.)

Integrating Information into the Decision-Making Process

"After clients get the information from us," Hill says, "they don't always know what to do with it. You might give them a phenomenal mailing list of potential customers, but at this point they may need to employ a marketing or management consultant who specializes in marketing or strategic analysis or competitive intelligence, and who can take the information, translate it, and explain how to use it for specific decision-making purposes."

Consulting-oriented services are now being developed at the Ben Franklin Technology Center within the Business Information Center. These functions, to translate and integrate information into the decision-making process, have historically been the realm of the state's small business development centers and private consultants. But the information specialists at the Business Center are helping to bridge the gap by leading small businesses in the right direction. "It's more than an educational process. It's actually effecting a change in behavior of business people who have been doing it one way." Hill finds herself telling clients that, "You are not going to be successful unless you use this new, high-technology system." She recalls one client who did not even have a PC on his desk when he discovered the BIC's service: "He thought he had found the Holy Grail. And that's exciting for us as information specialists as well."

Achieving Their Goals

This unique, government-supported program at the Ben Franklin Business Information Center provides information and helps businesses to make more informed decisions, and it is now recognized as a key tool in the economic development process. Marjorie Hill believed this when she joined the organization, but knew that she would have to start from scratch to introduce such new ideas of information retrieval to her clients. Working with businesses has helped her validate her prior experience and belief that many executives still do not recognize the value of information or business intelligence. She also anticipated, as a result of prior experiences, that it would be a battle to prove that the online information skills she possessed would be not only highly specialized but valuable to executives who needed information. Only since the emergence of the Internet are others beginning to realize what Hill and her staff have been saying from the beginning.

Over the years, however, Hill has discovered one technique in online demonstrations to get her clients interested and hold their attention: "You locate the name of the person you are trying to impress, or their organization, or their boss, in an online article. Then you project it on the screen using an overhead panel. You suddenly have their complete and absolute concentration. You personalize it. That gets them every time."

Adapting to Change

New programs are under consideration at the Ben Franklin Partnership and within the Business Information Center, as businesses now move further into the knowledge economy. For current information and links to the Business Information Center, visit the Web site at http://www.benfranklin.org/.

For More Information

I.   Electronic and Internet resources used for clients at the Business
     Information Center according to Marjorie Hill:

Besides a few key directories, such as Gale's *Manufacturing USA*, *Market Share Reporter*, and *Encyclopedia of Associations*, clients won't find the BIC staff using many print resources housed in this center. Nor will they find the staff using many consumer-oriented, menu-based, online systems, such as Prodigy or America Online. What they will find in the Business Information Center are search manuals for over 25 commercial online "robust" systems, such as Knight-Ridder's DIALOG® Information Services, Dow Jones News Retrieval, and LEXIS-NEXIS, and on smaller scale specialized systems, such as Knowledge Express, a database with access to federal, university, and private sector technology opportunities, and Community of Science, which provides access to academic researchers around the world. In total, BIC has access to over 4,000 database files from within these systems, and a search often scans 100 databases at a time just to glean an important fact or citation.

The top business-oriented database files that the center's information specialists search are ABI/INFORM, American Business Directory, Biobusiness, PR Newswire, Business Dateline, Business-wire, Commerce Business Daily, Disclosure Online, Dun & Bradstreet Credit Reports, Dun's Market Identifiers, International Dun's Market Identifiers, Investext, Legal Resource Index, Magazine Index, Moody's Corporate Reports, Piers Exports and Piers Imports, IAC PROMT, Thomas Register Online, Trade & Industry Database, Trademarkscan Federal and World Patents Index.

The top technology-oriented databases that may be used are Ei Compendex Plus, INSPEC, Ceramic Abstracts, Medline, Embase, Food Science and Technology Abstracts, and IAC Newsletter Database.

International databases include D&B International Market Identifiers, Corporate Affiliations, Financial Times Full Text, Israel Commercial Economic Newsletter, Euromonitor, Globalbase, the Wall Street Journal Europe, the Asian Wall Street Journal, and Agence France Presse English Wire.

Since 1995, BIC has had access to the Internet. The BIC staff, however, access it primarily as a supplement to research projects, adding to the results from commercial databases.

For professional searches, the Internet can be more trouble than tribute to this technology. Clients can't seem to fathom that commercial databases charging hundreds of dollars per hour for information are not available "for free" on the Internet. Nor do they understand that there are significant hidden costs on the Net, i.e., the long time it may take to find the information that leads to searches that may be more costly than the same search completed using commercial databases.

The Internet, in our opinion, will continue its phenomenal growth and provide an excellent new medium for access to primary information, but commercial vendors will continue to be dominant in providing secondary information retrieval.

This trend will be even more pronounced after Internet access is available through other information appliances such as television.

We think, at this point, that the Internet is a good place to look for information but not the best place to find information for making significant decisions. In addition, verification of the source of information can be very difficult on the Internet, which could have disastrous consequences for the user.

Often, clients either aren't aware of or have difficulty understanding the problems that we see. Opening the Internet to all has complicated our professional work with clients rather than helped, and there is more to come as access continues its global explosion.

II. Example that illustrates the value of a complex search statement and the results it can yield:

Topic: A BIC client asked to locate an industry discussion of how much it would cost oil and shipping companies if the law required double hulls for oil tankers.

Outcome: The outcome would provide full-text information that would enable the client to quickly become familiar with the current regulatory environment, key players, and contacts at the time.

Online Database System Used: Knight-Ridder's DIALOG® Information Services

Database Files Chosen: A search was conducted simultaneously across four database files that were thought to contain the most relevant information on the shipping industry and its regulatory environment. The files were the Journal of Commerce, McGraw Hill

Publications Online, IAC Newsletter Database, and IAC Trade &
Industry Database.

Sample Search Statement: The search statement below takes
advantage of a number of techniques to yield the precise information required from the four full-text database files. The techniques
used (in the vernacular of online searching) that tell DIALOG®'s
system what to do:

- truncation—a question mark (?) at the end of the word to
  retrieve its plural or other variations.
- proximity operators—a (W) which requires adjacency of
  words in the order specified; an (S) which requires that all of
  the words appear in the same paragraph.
- boolean operator—(OR) to combine synonyms and related
  terms into one concept statement.
- nesting—a combination search logic that allows for searching
  and combining terms in a single command string rather than
  in a series of separate steps by using parentheses to show
  what order words or terms should be searched and the relationships the various terms have to each other, thus saving
  time in the overall search.

The search statement was:

SS (SELECT STEPS)
TANKER?(S)DOUBLE(W)HULL(?)(LAW? OR
LEGAL? OR REGULAT?)(S)(COST? OR EXPEN?)

Sample Result: The search statement yielded 47 citations from the
four database files searched.

Here is one sample from the Trade & Industry Database by Wayne K.
Talley, professor of economics at Old Dominion University that
contained results of a 17-page study from *Logistics and Transportation Review* (Canada). Using the K or "kwic" (key word in
context) format allows a preliminary view (initially more
economical) of the words in context in the record:

Vessel damage severity of tanker accidents.

The release of nearly 11 million gallons of oil in Prince William Sound, Alaska, following the March 1989 grounding of the tanker vessel, the EXXON VALDEZ, was the impetus for passage of the Oil Pollution Act of 1990 by the United States (U.S.) Congress. The Act sought to reduce the oil pollution of tanker accidents by reducing their vessel damage (as opposed to reducing the number of tanker accidents) by mandating double hulls for tankers traveling in the U.S. waters by the year 2015. Proponents of double hulls argue that by adding a second hull on the bottom and sides of tankers, oil spills from grounding and collision accidents would be reduced. A National Research Council study (1991, p. 3) estimates that if tankers have double hulls, approximately half of the current annual average oil spillage in U.S. waters from tanker collision and grounding accidents would be saved. Critics argue that the extra protection is not cost effective: Hopkins (1992, p. 59) concludes that "costs appear substantial relative to benefits, and lawmakers' emphasis on design standards deflects attention from alternative risk reduction strategies—e.g., operation and maintenance measures that warrant equal attention.

The Oil and Pollution Act of 1990 may have correctly focused on the policy of vessel design (i.e., double hulls) as an effective policy for reducing the vessel damage severity (and the subsequent oil spillage) of collision tanker accidents.

By contrast, a number of hypothesized, explanatory variables were statistically significant in our grounding tanker accident estimations: vessel size with a negative coefficient, suggesting...

Cost of a Typical Search: $300 to $500, which includes amount of time to formulate search strategy and conduct the search, as well as the online database costs (whether the citations were full-text, or summaries were also factors in cost).

(Permission to reprint granted by National Technical Information Service and DIALOG® Information Services/Knight-Ridder, Inc.)

III.   More About the Ben Franklin Partnership:

In a 1992 survey of employment growth regions, *Business Week* (19 October, p. 80) praised the significant role state governments have played in supporting new job creation and recognized the Ben Franklin/IRC Partnership (a Commonwealth of Pennsylvania program that funds the Ben Franklin Technology Centers) as the "granddaddy" of state development programs. And David Osborne, the coauthor of the widely cited *Reinventing Government* (Addison-Wesley, 1992), described the Ben Franklin Partnership in his first book, *Laboratories of Democracy* (Harvard Business School Press, 1988), as "arguably the best state economic development program in the country."

When it was created in 1982, a significant component of the Ben Franklin Partnership Program was the establishment of four Advanced Technology Centers located across the state that would form strategic partnerships with public, private, and academic organizations to provide financing and services for technology-based and growth-oriented companies.

According to the Partnership's ten-year report released at the end of 1993, the positive impact of the Centers' projects on economic development in Pennsylvania was impressive: "Through 1991, the Partnership's four regional Technology Centers created and retained over 24,000 jobs, started and expanded 1,800 new companies, commercialized 540 products and processes, and leveraged over $750 million in nonstate funds." The report also said that in ten years, the Technology Center program has successfully transformed Pennsylvania from a 'rustbelt' state dominated by large manufacturers, to a diversified economy populated by small, high-tech enterprises and has provided a model for the development of an effective and entrepreneurial national economic development policy."

As it begins its second decade of service, the Ben Franklin Technology Center program has evolved to meet the changing needs of the Pennsylvania economy, and by the end of 1995, it was reported by Marjorie Hill that "over 80 percent of funded companies continue to survive and employ over 6,000 local residents and have led to 116 commercialized products."

Here is a list of the services provided at Ben Franklin Technology Centers:

Financing: covers due diligence and technical assistance for product development and commercialization of early stage technology companies and microloans to low-income women and minority entrepreneurs.

Services: unique one-stop shopping for the entrepreneurial community, including:

- Technology assessments and opportunities to commercialize technologies that originate in the region's universities
- Centers of research excellence that give access to world-class university faculty and facilities
- Total quality management consortiums provided by community colleges and regional chambers of commerce; regional export consortiums to define export opportunities
- Job-link programs to train welfare recipients for employment in targeted industries
- A Small Business Investment Research (SBIR) office for small businesses engaged in product research and development
- Small business incubators that provide space and business development assistance
- Technology access services to assist defense-dependent companies in developing products for nonmilitary applications
- The Business Information Center (BIC) providing small to midsized companies with timely technology, market, industry, and competitive information through access to online electronic databases

Chapter 9 A Manager of a Multinational Corporate Information Center

Daan Boom

> For knowledge companies such as KPMG the only sustainable competitive advantage will become the ability to learn. A key characteristic of OpenAccess knowledge infrastructure is that it supports the ability to acquire knowledge, enhance it, store it in an organized way, and make it accessible to everyone who needs it within our firm.
>
> Daan Boom

"Our company's assets reside in the knowledge of our people," says Daan Boom, manager of the Informatie & Research Centrum for KPMG in Amsterdam. It is Boom's job to serve his company's knowledge workers who consist of approximately 3,800 "highly educated people," i.e., the KPMG accountants and consultants who need information for themselves and their clients within the Netherlands and Belgium.

The KPMG Profile

The company Boom works for is an international accounting and consulting firm serving multinational companies, such as Aetna, Apple Computer, Citicorp, Motorola, Siemens, U.S. Airways, and Xerox. It was formed in 1987 as the result of a merger of Peat Marwick of the United States and Klynveld Main Goerdeler, Europe's largest accounting firm. The merger moved KPMG into the first position in the world among accounting firms at that time. In 1996, the firm had 6,100 partners and 76,200 total personnel in Africa, Asia, Europe, the Middle East, North America, and Latin America with offices in 819 cities in 125 countries. Worldwide, income from fees was $6.1 billion. In the United States, KPMG competes with the big six accounting/consulting firms: Arthur Anderson, Coopers & Lybrand, Deloitte & Touche, Ernst & Young, H&R Block, Marsh & McLennan, McKinsey & Co., and Price Waterhouse. KPMG provides auditing, accounting, and tax services, as well as consulting services and corporate finance services for mergers and acquisitions. Key areas of expertise worldwide include financial services, government services, health care and life sciences, information and communications, manufacturing, retailing, and distribution.

Daan Boom's Profile

Daan Boom earned a degree in library and archive science, followed by advanced courses in informatics and economics in the Netherlands. That was 15 years ago. "The technology is changing now so dramatically that it is not possible to look back even five years," says Boom. But he thinks it was important for him to take the informatics courses to learn how databases are structured and to obtain his economics degree in order to manage the business side of the information and research center.

Defining Levels of Information
Service and Support at KPMG

"Within the information structure of KPMG in the Netherlands, and I think it is quite similar in all of our centers," says Boom, "we have been providing our users mainly two levels of tasks associated with our information center. The first level is what we call the 'librarian' task which is buying and cataloging books, indexing journals, distributing journals for associates, all the standard work of an information center. A lot of what we are providing (like basic information services) is still important. Our librarians know how to buy a book, at which book store, and how to get the best quality discount, services that the end user is expecting. But if you want to distinguish yourself as a real professional, you should add something else. Everybody expects an information professional to deliver a book within a week or two."

Boom explains that the second level of task provided and marketed within the information center is the information-providing service, what is called the "documentation" service. This level of service provides KPMG professionals, i.e., the accountants and consultants (what he calls the "fee-earners" within the company) with the data and information they need in a ready-to-use format.

Boom continues:

> It used to be that our accountants and consultants would ask questions such as, "Do you have any information about treasury management or software packages?" We would provide them with a list (bibliography) of references, and they could make a choice out of that, or we could then provide them with the full article. Or, if a question came in about the stock market prices of a certain company in New York, we would look through the electronic databases or printed resources and give them the answer.

Boom explains that this standard documentation service, answering the quick and dirty questions or simple fact checking, is still an important part of the service, but the accountants and consultants have begun to request information that they can use directly in their reports. The process requires an expansion of the skills of Boom's experienced searcher staff and includes the ability to provide search results that are manipulated through analysis to the extent that value is added to the raw information retrieved online.

Prior to 1993, spending more than one hour on a certain task was considered "not done." Boom says that the information center's task was to "rush and give them the information and hop to the next question." But that task is changing very rapidly.

Providing Strategic Planning Support

The emergence of information professionals in the corporate strategic planning process began during a downsizing period of the company when Boom was told that his staff in the information center had to develop and deliver more than the standard perceived level of service. He was told that they must present themselves as information professionals with high value to the company or the service itself would begin to outsource to information providers and services.

A third level of support was then initiated, strategic planning support. Boom says that up to this point it had taken a long time for this information service to be recognized for its business potential within the organization and that "it was partly due to the fact that the information professionals had not been trained to communicate with professionals on their level and to understand their basic information needs."

Making Librarians Business Literate

It seemed that while the librarians of the information center were highly information literate, they were not entirely business literate, nor were they close enough to decision makers to know their information needs. Meeting the current information needs of KPMG's consultants required learning new skills, such as making spreadsheet programs or analyzing annual reports, skills most of the accountants and consultants at KPMG learned in college, i.e., MBA-type skills, such as accounting and quantitative analysis.

To meet these new demands, Boom organized computer and business training sessions for key library staff. "I think it is easier to train a consultant in the information skills than to train a librarian in business and analytic skills," he says. "It is partly because the consultants and accountants are trained in what we call in economics the B level, where they know mathematics, whereas the librarians are trained more or less in what is called A level, a language level where mathematical skills are not necessary for understanding the theoretical background." However, Boom also notes that while it is possible to train the consultants to become end users, it may not be at the same skill level that information professionals are trained to provide.

Being Put to the Test

To test the newly acquired business skills and to prove that they could do the kind of work required, Boom's staff of information professionals initially chose to work with the merger and acquisition consultants under corporate finance. He describes the process: "Even if it cost us extra hours or working on Saturdays or Sundays, we didn't mind because we could compensate through the week. Sometimes it happened that we worked in the evening or the weekends. We just wanted to keep on going. And it has worked very, very well."

A project Boom cites proudly was the identification of potential acquisition candidates within Europe for a U.S. client who wanted to start a business in Europe. There were two options: "One was to start a factory somewhere in Europe; the other was to try to form an alliance or takeover using the same management structure with a company that had the same distribution facilities within Europe. The acquisition candidate should give the client large quantities of products to be distributed all over Western Europe."

Boom's team reviewed the request and made a long list of European candidates that fell within certain parameters, such as assets and turnover. For example, "ideal candidates shouldn't be larger in sales than the U.S. client, could be at least a little bit smaller, should have modern equipment, and should have modality access of waterways and transport areas." Based on those first qualifiers, Boom and his team identified ideal candidates, categorized them by country, and provided basic information, such as a short description of their activities. The team also analyzed what they call the "mother and daughter" relations the firm already had along with information about their strength. The long list identified approximately 65 companies.

The team of consultants then discussed the information with the client based on what Boom's team provided, which included detailed profiles of 20 companies, three from each country.

Here is a recap of the resources used:

The long list was compiled from *Dun & Bradstreet* information about different European countries. The team added additional data about the different companies, including product descriptions, gathered through local directory sources. They used *ABC* for German companies, *Kompass* for those in the U.K., and the French directory *Delphes* for French companies. Financial information, if not provided by the *Dun & Bradstreet* database of marketing identifiers, was gathered from Bureau van Diik's CD Collection of European Companies (Amadeus) and from local Chambers of Commerce. They also used *Profiles* (McCarthy) and *Reuters* for a "few lines of text" if companies had been covered in journals or newspapers in the last couple of years.

The second stage required more detailed research. Boom's team went back to *Reuters* and local databases for company information, the long credit ratings in *Dun & Bradstreet,* and *Extel, ICC, PROMT,* and *McCarthy* for news clipping databases with European coverage. They also sent e-mail messages to the European KPMG Global Information Network (GIN) to request information about published annual reports.

The result of this research generated almost three pages of text abstracted from the sources of information Boom's team had gathered—additional financial information, annual reports over the last three years, and more data on the company itself, that is, who were the suppliers and to whom were they supplying.

"About 20 companies were targeted," says Boom. "On about 16 or 17, we had pretty good background information, and on about six companies the information was pretty poor. But still the candidate looked pretty good, so at that level, the information was provided to corporate finance, where they started the process of entering financial data into spreadsheet programs and creating stats and graphical information about the company, its competition, and its products."

At this point, it was out of the hands of Boom's team. After discussing the different opportunities with the client, the ten remaining companies were accessed by the corporate finance department to evaluate possibilities.

Passing the Test

In taking the opportunity to prove their worth, Boom's team became the "first line of defense," screening companies from a long list to a short list for further action by the merger and acquisition team.

Feedback about their work came to the Boom team after the deal itself had been finalized when the U.S. client actually took over the European company. Boom and his colleagues went with the KPMG team from the United States, the people from the acquired company, and the corporate finance consultants "to the theater and dinner just to celebrate within a small group. And we got a sort of diploma as a reward. It was very encouraging to be made a part of the team," says Boom.

News of the value-added work created in the information center spread around to other centers at KPMG in the Netherlands, as their graphics and research results began to appear in client's reports. Those kinds of reports were discussed among the consultants, who would say, "Hey, how did you get those graphics?" and "That's nice and looks very good." They began to recognize that this was information provided by the information center, and then "they began to recognize that we have the staff and facilities to do those things," Boom remarks.

"If they are asking for information to compare two or three companies in a benchmarking process, for instance, and we are showing that we can calculate what we call betas or performance indicators and provide some background information in a very descriptive form of business activity and then put it in a scheme or a graphic, then they will reward us very highly by recognizing our services and resources as a valuable asset for the company," he explains.

New Information Products

More recently, Boom and his team have developed more sophisticated, value-added information products:

> As part of the exercise mentioned above, we have optimized the company search process in a detailed checklist of steps to undertake if a company or sector profile is needed. We now delegate the information-gathering process to an information assistant and do the synthesizing by an experienced information professional. We are now able to offer "our clients" a pretty well priced information package on a company with basic financials, up to five competitor profiles with basic benchmarking information, and a more cost-effective information package with more detailed information. These information packages are divided into easy access chapters and in binder format, and are very successful and have had a very positive effect on the image of the Information Centre.

The Information Professionals
as Consultants to the Consultants

Now, more than before, Boom's information team is being asked to join project teams. "From the first meeting where the task is divided, it is decided what kind of information will be needed, who is doing what, and what cost could be involved. And the information professional has the job to stick up his/her hand and say that is an information problem and 'We can handle that,'" Boom says.

In some cases, the consultants have begun to look to the information professionals to take the lead in determining what information will be needed to get the job done, because they are more familiar with the information resources.

The Global Information Network (GIN)—Linking KPMG's Information Centers Worldwide

Two other programs have been developed that attest to the proactive stance adapted by corporate librarians at KPMG, both in the information center in Amsterdam and in other KPMG information centers worldwide. Both are being developed under the umbrella of "OpenAccess." The first program is called the Global Information Network (GIN), drafted to create an information-gathering tool by linking KPMG information centers and its information professionals worldwide. "Within each GIN, we are making use of local knowledge to access local information," says Boom. "That means that if the librarians in New York need information about a Dutch or European company, they can contact us through e-mail directly, and we will find it for them and send it by express, fax, or e-mail."

Daan Boom says that the original business plan for GIN was created to provide the connection between quality information services and the values and strategic goals of KPMG International. The plan presented information as a commodity, and information storage and retrieval as a business where information specialists served as consultants and operated on a cost recovery basis. Boom explains: "The writers of the plan wanted the company to appreciate the resources already available from the libraries, and beyond this, they wanted support for expanding the libraries' mission and resources. The motto became: 'We have the people, we have the tools; as a team we can do the job.'"

A key benefit the GIN now offers to KPMG is to place the most advanced information and technology at the disposal of many of the company's far-flung locations. The network enables the information professionals to encourage a more efficient level of operation by identifying and providing common solutions, standardizing hardware and software, and negotiating agreements with database vendors for cost-effective pricing.

Other potential benefits of the network are that the libraries in the network can generate revenue for the organization, both by billing current clients and by carrying out projects for others. Resource sharing also saves money for the firm.

Knowing the Content

Boom explains that the GIN is now recognized by top management as a very valuable asset and as a powerful worldwide information resource and service for the firm. Top management also recognizes the information specialists throughout the network for their extensive knowledge of and expertise with content, thus enabling access not only to global sources but especially to reliable local data, such as statistics about a country's economy, including population and economic growth, inflation, labor costs, trade, and current account. "This information is not retrieved from directories that provide this kind of information of a few years ago, but from the most up-to-date sources," says Boom.

The development and growth of the GIN is the result of a worldwide cooperative effort by all GIN members who meet and provide feedback on an ongoing basis about relevant sources used or needed to conduct business in their respective countries. One of the results of the collaboration is the ongoing fine-tuning of the system to provide more efficient access and use to all of the available resources. "For example," says Boom, "lists ranking critical external information providers have been derived and pursued. For instance, we identified five categories of information that supports our line of business, the function, and service in which our professionals serve. Although these types of information categories may be similar, the sources that support them may vary from country to country based on reliability, delivery, and credibility."

"The GIN is an example of information professionals taking the initiative in playing an active role in their company's globalization of operations. They are using the strategic management concepts learned in working in a consulting environment, and the tremendous potential of new technologies to develop their vision into a reality," Boom says proudly.

KPMG's Intranet—Linking
KPMG's Consulting and
Accounting Practices

As technology has evolved enabling electronic exchange of information worldwide (the Internet) and corporatewide (the Intranet), Boom explains the development and implementation of a second project under the KPMG OpenAccess Program:

> In Wave I of KPMG's Intranet, the Dutch practice, KPMG in Amsterdam, developed in 1994 an entirely new knowledge infrastructure based upon web technology called DOKOS, "Documentation and Knowledge Communication System." In the Netherlands and even in Europe, it was the first Intranet application by a non-IT firm. In November 1996, Wave II was introduced, connecting KPMG practices in the U.K., U.S., and Canada using standard Internet technology to create their own internal, enterprise-wide web, also known as OpenAccess. Further introduction to implement this communication and information-sharing system within KPMG are being realized. Although OpenAccess is the global name for this project, local practices have their own names for their Intranets: DOKOS for the Netherlands, K-Man for the U.S., Intraweb for Canada, and U-Know for the U.K.

"OpenAccess now links local Intranet solutions to deliver a seamless interface that provides access to important databases, competitive data, external research resources, newsfeeds, and more from points around the globe," says Boom. For instance, users would be able to access the *Wall Street Journal*, and the *Financial Times*, as well as have e-mail capabilities and new services as they developed.

Boom explains that when DOKOS was under development, it was necessary to determine the information needs of accountants and consultants. The result was a series of interviews and questionnaires. Following the interviews, the company decided to create a table of contents menu consisting of the following topics:

(1)   Business and European community law
(2)   Accounting requirements (Dutch and U.S.)
(3)   Taxes
(4)   Social securities
(5)   KPMG internal know-how

(6)   Business sections which include
    (a)   Economic figures
    (b)   Financial dailies (newspapers)
    (c)   Market information

Each category was chosen with the needs of the company in mind and is expected to prove invaluable in the development and maintenance of the corporate knowledge bases of KPMG's employees, i.e., the intellectual capital of the company.

Basic requirements for creating and maintaining the system specified that Boom and his staff would prepare, edit, and mount the data; that it would have an easy search engine (for Mac and Windows); and that it would be cost effective. The browser chosen was Netscape because of its open architecture. Netscape supports all different search engines to be used within OpenAccess and DOKOS. Currently, several text-search engines such as Excalibur, Verity, and Personal Librarian, are being explored.

Boom explains that all members of the GIN network played a significant role in the adoption of the corporatewide Intranet program called DOKOS and all reviewed valuable sources to be incorporated. As part of that, it is recognized that KPMG information professionals will implement their own homepages within the OpenAccess project. On these pages, valuable local sources will be accessible, such as local stock exchange quotations and interest rates.

Many changes have occurred at KPMG in Amsterdam, and particularly in the information center. Daan Boom led his professional staff to adopt the technologies needed to bring the company into the electronic information age, and he has guided them in learning the skills that will not only provide information but enhance the work of the teams along the way. When asked what Boom would consider his ideal information environment, he replies:

> I would like to see more end users who are able to find information on their own to free us to do evaluative and analytical work. Getting DOKOS alive is a great achievement in allowing this to happen. The next challenge we will face as KPMG information professionals is to organize the integration of the various internal knowledge resources which turns knowledge into value for the benefit of its clients, its people, and its communities.

Daan Boom

For More Information

For access to the corporate homepage of KPMG, go to http://www.kpmg.com.

(Note: At publication time for *InfoThink*, a merger of KPMG and Ernst & Young was announced. For Ernst & Young's homepage, go to http://www.ey.com.)

Chapter 10   A Knowledge Analyst

Denise Cumming

> Yes, there is a world of information available online, and it is, in a manner of speaking, at your fingertips. But there's quite a bit more to it than that. Online searching may not be rocket science, but it does take a little more knowledge and intellectual effort than bungee jumping. Sometimes, come to think of it, it feels like a combination of the two."
>
> Reva Basch, *Secrets of the Supersearchers,*
> *The Accumulated Wisdom of 23 of the World's*
> *Top Online Searchers,* 1993

Denise Cumming is a hard-core infopro who would like to dispel the myth that information is easy to access. She says some people actually believe the machine (i.e., the computer and software) can do things that they think are easy "because there is a big misunderstanding about what information people do." And Cumming says that there is a belief that a machine can replace information people because they think that "what they do is not difficult, not complex, not brainwork, not human, and because of that...they think computers can do it."

Intelligent Agents: Secretaries,
Information Specialists, and
Investment Advisors

The idea of intelligent agents in the workplace (sometimes called man-machine systems in early research) has captured the imagination of scientists worldwide. Over the past 30 years, important research has been conducted about how humans think and about how computers might be made to think like humans (i.e., artificial intelligence [AI]). Areas such as linguistics, cognitive sciences, social sciences, and the information sciences all have an artificial intelligence component. In 1994, Marina Roesler and Donald T. Hawkins of AT&T Bell Laboratories said in an article about intelligent agents in *Online,*[1] "Intelligent agents could play the roles of a highly competent secretary, reference librarian, personal and relentless world events watcher, news-clip agency, office and personal "gopher," personal shopper, personal investment advisor, or decision-making counselor. These capabilities, of indisputable value, will bring about a welcomed service-model shift that we can expect will touch and shape all of our lives significantly."

Cumming, the Knowledge Analyst

Denise Cumming has an informed viewpoint about using intelligent agents and knowbots for information retrieval, because she has worked with scientists, engineers, chemists, and patent attorneys throughout her career. She began with ten years at Honeywell, Inc. in Minneapolis in the mid-1970s, where she created and managed information services for the Technology Strategy Center, and then at Teltech, Inc., a technical knowledge service in Minneapolis.

Her own boss now, Cumming's matter-of-fact views about the use of information in technical and business settings are influenced by her experiences as a designated "knowledge analyst" on the staff during Teltech's infancy. While there, she worked on a team with other information professionals who sorted through hundreds of electronic databases to find the precise information needed in such subject areas as aerospace, chemicals, electronics, computers, and pharmaceuticals. She helped develop and utilize the interactive (real-time) search service that provided leading-edge data from the scientific and technical literature to Teltech's corporate clients—senior technical people, directors of research, project managers, and vice presidents for research and development (R&D) or engineering.

An Endangered Species

Cumming thinks it is important that the skills of the information specialist be recognized within the organization and in the business world. Many times throughout her career, she has had to define and defend her turf as a professional online searcher. She says that such specialists are in trouble because there is a lack of understanding by end users and decision makers of what they can do, and many companies have let them go, leaving no one in the company who knows how to think about information. As she observes:

> There is a shortage of skilled knowledge analysts/information specialists/librarians (or whatever they should be called). We need as many librarians as we now have. If you took all the technical people in the country, you need one in ten librarians—not the old-fashioned kind of librarian, i.e., "guarding the books"; you need thousands of information people to be helpers and guides to act as a bridge to the information. Perhaps it will have to be another specialty. They will need, at a minimum, the things that a good, solid undergraduate education can give, i.e., a big vocabulary, a lot of communication skills, flexibility, a good analytical mind, and the ability to deal with ambiguity.

Supersearchers Versus MBAs

Cumming believes that big companies presently pay MBAs a lot of money right out of school because they think they are valuable. "But they aren't good at information," she says. "They might be good at finding company information that relates to a specific area because that's how they are trained. But, in fact, MBAs might learn a few tricks from experienced information people. One thing they might learn is that good information people help the expensive people, the ones with the big technical brain or the big business brain who should not be wasting their expensive time searching for information anywhere!—especially on the Internet."

Firing the Chefs

"Over the last ten years, corporate America has laid off incredibly good information/library talent," she continues:

> For 20 years, information specialists and librarians have been getting better and more sophisticated. Corporations were giving them golden parachutes, because they didn't want to pay for them anymore even though the librarians were a lot cheaper than the engineers, than MBAs, and management. Yet they were laying off these highly skilled librarians, and there's no talent to replace them because information skills are not easy or inexpensive skills to acquire. They don't know the skill exists; therefore, they don't know it is in short supply and that it is not easy to create or buy in the marketplace. Corporations and organizations are just beginning to realize that you can't replace these kinds of skills with a computer or machine or buy it in the marketplace.

In her style, Cumming says, "And now, just when the food trucks are coming down the (information) highway, they are firing all the chefs!"

Answering Business Questions

Cumming describes the kinds of business questions she helped Teltech clients answer:

> Business people asked very similar questions over and over. They had a formula question with an x factor in it. For example, what is the market share for *xyz*? Who is *xyz* company? If it was something like IBM, a broad publicly held company, you got too much, if it was "Denise's Search Farm," you got "0." Business questions are somewhat redundant. There's either too much or too little information. Big companies have so much information you can't deal with it; small, privately held companies or subsidiaries, which are even harder to understand, are difficult to find information on at all.

Answering Scientific and Technical Questions

"Science is different," says Cumming.

Scientific information retrieval can't be simplified; it is too technical. For example: What is the difference between the American Petroleum Institute database for oil and the Tulsa database from the University of Oklahoma for oil? Which one would you go to if you were interested in oil? Tulsa's database is information before the wellhead—looking for it, exploring for it, asking what kind of geology it is in, how you dig a hole, how you bring it up to the wellhead and pipe it over to the refinery. The American Petroleum Institute database is information from the refinery on, after the wellhead. Now, that's esoteric information of the highest order, and you can't make a machine that can know how to ask those necessary questions to direct someone to the correct database. And how do you get a machine to ask questions from all the other databases, such as the electrical engineering database, the chemical databases, right behind them are the metallurgical databases, behind that is Inspec and Engineering Index, the engineering databases, and then the plastics and rubber databases, the inks, paints, and aluminum? These databases exist because there is that much information on each subject!

One Size Can't Fit All

Cumming says that while software can be programmed to find information, "One size can't fit all. Never! Ever! And I believe that until you understand pretty deeply about information, you do not understand why that is true. The reason you can't make it easy is because you are dealing with two things that are not machinable." She continues:

One is language, i.e., the same word means different things in different contexts, with nuances and embedded meanings. And even if you have the biggest computer in the world, it is almost impossible to guess in advance all of the contexts. You would have to be able to anticipate the majority of the questions in the universe in order to design a machine that will work for people who have the questions. If you don't have the questions, you can't do it.

Denise Cumming admits that language is not her specialty, but since she has been answering those questions for 20 years, she has an idea what the most popular and relevant questions are. "And of course, that's how you would design your system," she says.

Simulating Human Intelligence

"The second reason you can't program software to find information," says Cumming, "is because human intelligence is a process that is hard to simulate." For instance, she says:

> Not to say that you can't simulate parts of it, little pieces that are simplistic. The only way you can find out those little pieces is by studying how people communicate about their information needs [and there are people studying these]. But it can't be one size fits all. It can be very sophisticated *if* it is on a very narrow subject. In fact, the narrower the subject, the higher percentage of useful information very naive people would get from the system. Airline reservation systems are an example. If the subject area is wide, you can't anticipate all of the questions that might be connected with that broad area of information. The non-information person does not find it easy to imagine other people's questions. But the skilled information person knows there could be 50 ways to ask the question, that they come in many varieties. Your customer may say "I don't know how to ask..." They see it only in one path, but it is a tiny thread in a whole web. It is only the person who experiences a broad variety of different uses of questions who can help you see that one size will never fit all. Because of this, it is extremely hard to turn the information-seeking process into a mass consumption product.

Scientists (and Executives) Are Not Using the Best Information

"We seem to have this tremendous paradox in the U.S.," Cumming observes:

> Because of the rush for the moon in the '60s, we invented, housed, and organized the world's best research in databases, and we have been managing to continue to maintain these databases, and it's

still the cheapest, best access to information (in the world). How else are you going to look at eight million references from Chemical Abstracts? Even if it does cost you $3 per minute, it's still much cheaper than hiring someone to look through an index in a print version of Chemical Abstracts in the library. And the paradox is that even though we invented it here, the executives (i.e., decision makers in companies) aren't aware of it and the scientists are not using it.

NTIS: A National Treasure

Cumming thinks that there should be much more attention paid to our national scientific and corporate knowledge bases. She cites an example:

We are not even using the information we own in the National Technical Information Service (NTIS),[2] even though the documents one can get through NTIS are incredibly valuable. It is very good information, and it's very cheap. It goes back to 1964 and is comprised of the basic government-sponsored research 10-15 years before it was even considered in the marketplace. That's why I consider it a national treasure, because we did a lot of research back when we were willing to spend money on government research. We could use that research and now make new products if we would go back and look at it. Some people who have looked at it are shocked to learn that important work was done 30 years ago. We are not even treating it like the national jewel that it is. It's incredibly cheap when you think that you can call them up, give them a credit card number, and get a government document of high technical value for $25 in the mail two days later! But no one knows i'ts there, and no one knows how to get it. And very few people who have power in companies know where the good information is.

(See For More Information for sample NTIS citations to early research on artificial intelligence.)

The Simultaneous Remote Search:
Helping Scientists (and Executives)
Find and Use Information

A number of experiments were conducted in the scientific and technical community in the 1970s, when online searching was in its infancy, to develop more user-friendly methods because usage had been slow to catch on except in a relatively small segment of those in business and industry. Some of the reasons for this were mentioned in an article describing a model experiment conducted in Eastern Oregon. In the 1987 "The Eastern Oregon Information Network," Verl A. Anderson listed some common problems that dispel the myth of easy information access:

- All systems are not the same
- Telecommunications skills are not common
- All individuals who access the systems do not all have the same degree of success
- Often, end users can't express their information needs in words that allow the system to retrieve the information.[3]

Anderson's article also describes the Simultaneous Remote Search (SRS) implemented by medical librarians in Oregon to help practicing physicians in isolated rural environments get access to current medical literature. Results of the project showed that Simultaneous Remote Searching yields a current reality: that the librarian is still an interface agent between the end user and the knowledge base.

Cumming points to even earlier experiments and studies of the benefits of the SRS process. In 1977, an extensive survey of technical and R&D communities was conducted by the NASA Industrial Application Center (NASA/IAC) at the University of Southern California to determine the costs and benefits of online literature searches.[4] The results helped to validate the importance of the interactive search process, in which the client is present or in close communication and totally involved in determining the information needed.

This process evolved to commercial use in the mid-1980s when Teltech, Inc. utilized it as part of the service they offered to their clients. "Expert Systems the Old-Fashioned Way: Person to Person,"[5] an article in *Online* in 1988, described interactive literature searching at the company. Cumming, who was active in its implementation while at Teltech, explains how it actually worked:

Clients (mainly scientific or technical researchers) would call an 800 number, discuss their search topics, then decide whether they wanted to conduct the search interactively or have it mailed or faxed to them. If they decide on an interactive search, there is then a thorough interview to clarify the topic in order to understand the specific question. The knowledge analyst talks the client through the communications software to establish the modem-to-modem connection. Then as the literature search is underway, it is simulcast directly to the client's PC monitor via a modem-to-modem connection. This direct communication between client and searcher during an interactive search allows for immediate client participation in judging what is important to retrieve from the electronic source. The client knows the subject matter—and the searcher knows the editorial focus of the various databases, along with their strengths and weaknesses. This then becomes a "thinking machine" for scientific users.

The software needed is any communications software that allows the computer to dial the phone and capture the data. The hardware needed is a computer, two telephone lines at one end, and three telephone lines at the other end. And you need the "3D Switch" (a terminal-master slave [TMS] switch) at the searcher's end.

Cumming says that the greatest value in the interactive search is "just being able to help sort out the questions quickly as a result of showing the user examples of titles."

The searchee (researcher or client) wants to know everything about solar energy. And the searcher says: "Do you want terrestrial solar energy or space solar energy?" The searchee (he or she) didn't know before he asked the question that he has to make this decision first. He doesn't want everything about solar energy, he just wanted to build a single-family residence that uses solar energy to heat the air, not the water, and that's a lot different than using solar energy to send telecommunications back to earth from a satellite.

Some people say about online searching: "You have to know the right buzzwords," *but that's not it*...and that's why everybody thinks its easy. They think all you have to do is get the right word and then you push a button to get the right answer! But from the searcher's perspective, it requires cognitive understanding of the structure of the entire subject area or domain!

Cumming asks: "What happens when the information specialist can put in front of the eyes of the questioner a selection of good possibilities?" And here is her answer:

Suddenly this connects with what is already in his (or her) mind, and he starts to think about his question in a different way; it may change his approach to his question, because he is presented with possible solutions; he thinks about things he wouldn't have thought about before. It is in front of him in real life. There are articles about something that is pretty close to what he is working on, and now he can pick and say, "Well, actually, I'm not all that interested in the ones that are made with urea...I only want the ones that are made with ash." So then the information specialist, who knows how databases work, knows how to subtract out the urea ones without taking away the good ones, or knows how to tell him that he can't take the urea ones out, because he will throw out the baby with the bath. The information specialist would say: "Is it possible that there would be a good article comparing the urea ones to those with ash?" and he would say, "Yes, I really need the comparison."

Bingo! This was *never* previously communicated without the interaction between the searcher and the client—and the machine!

The Physics of Information

This is where the "physics of information" comes in, says Cumming:

All the computer is doing is matching up the shapes of the letters. Many people might think the computer is thinking about their question. If I type in "analysis," they think the computer is thinking of other similar words. They don't realize that the computer is a pattern recognition machine. The computer does an incredible job of finding the exact words and counting them up, unbelievably fast, but it is not thinking! What happens during an interactive search process is that the person with the question gets to think a lot faster about the question. It makes time collapse. You get to the good stuff faster—and cheaper!

A Special Padded Room—for Ultimate Productivity

Cumming believes that the interactive search process is "a new way on the planet" for technical people in particular. It's a new way to help them think about the questions:

"It's a dream lots of technical people have about the computer: They go into this special padded room that helps them think better' the computer will be nice, will talk to them, will understand them, will help them to be creative. And they don't have to push any buttons. It's the perfect 'AI' interface except the intelligence is *not* artificial—it's a human being, and it is the information specialist who is the perfect intelligent interface!"

Notes

1.   Marina Roesler and Donald T. Hawkins, "Intelligent Agents, Software Servants for an Electronic Information World (and More!)," *Online*, 18 July 1994, 18-32.

?   NTIS is a nonappropriated agency of the U.S. Department of Commerce's Technology Administration and an official resource for government-sponsored U.S. and worldwide scientific, technical, engineering, and business-related information. It provides access to more than two million documents, reports, studies, computer programs, and databases. The electronic collection goes back to the early sixties. To access the NTIS Web site, go to: http://www.ntis.gov.

3.   Verl A. Anderson, "The Eastern Oregon Information Network," *Library Hi Tech*, 2, no. 18 (Summer 1987): 66-67.

4.   Rebecca J. Jensen, Herbert O. Asbury, and Radford G. King, "Costs and Benefits to Industry of Online Literature Searches," *Special Libraries*, 71, no. 7 (July 1980): 291-298.

5.   Hunter McCleary and William J. Mayer, "Expert Systems the Old-Fashioned Way: Person to Person," *Online*, 2, no. 4 (July 1988): 15-24.

For More Information

I.   Some important ideas about artificial intelligence comes from Stephen Pinker, professor and director of the center for cognitive neuroscience at Massachusetts Institute of Technology and a leading linguistic researcher, who talks about artificial intelligence as it relates to language in *The Language Instinct, How the Mind Creates Language* (New York: William Morrow, 1994): 192-193.

For centuries, people have been terrified that their programmed creations might outsmart them, overpower them or put them out of work...When "artificial intelligence" (AI) was born in the 1950s it looked as though fiction was about to turn into frightening fact...But household robots are still confined to science fiction. The main lesson of 35 years of

AI research is that the hard problems are easy and the easy problems hard. The mental abilities of a four-year-old that we take for granted—recognizing a face, lifting a pencil, walking across a room, answering a question—in fact solve some of the hardest engineering problems ever created. Do not be fooled by the assembly-line robots in the automobile commercials; all they do is weld and spray-paint, tasks that do not require these clumsy Mr. Magoos to see or hold or place anything. And if you want to stump an artificial intelligence system, ask it questions like "Which is bigger, Chicago or a breadbox? Do zebras wear underwear? Is the floor likely to rise up and bite you?"...Understanding a sentence is one of these hard/easy problems. To interact with computers we still have to learn their languages—they are not smart enough to learn ours. In fact, it is all too easy to give computers more credit at understanding than they deserve.

II.   Following are several citations of titles from an online search conducted in the National Technical Information Service database on early research (1956-1965) in artificial intelligence:

- Strategies of Function Decomposition for Artificial Intelligence, Volume II
  (Final scientific rept. for Sep 64-Jun 65)
  Willis, David G.
  Computer Usage C Inc Palo Alto Calif
  1 Jul 65, 2p

- A Discussion of Artificial Intelligence and Self-Organization
  Pask, Gordon
  System Research Ltd Richmond (England)
  1964, 2p

- A Concise Bibliography of the Literature on Artificial Intelligence
  Pierce, Alice M.
  Air Force Cambridge Research Labs Bedford Mass
  Sep 59, 2p

- Three Branches of Artificial Intelligence Research
  (Professional paper)
  Hormann, Aiko
  System Development Corp Santa Monica Calif
  12 Nov 64, 2p

- A Review of the Field of Artificial Intelligence and Its Possible
  Applications to NASA Objectives, Final Report
  Pedelty, M. J.
  American University, Washington, DC, School of Government
  and Public Administration
  Feb 65, 19p

- Heuristic Aspects of the Artificial Intelligence Problem
  (Group report)
  Minsky, M. L.
  Lincoln Lab., Mass. Inst. of Tech., Lexington.
  17 Dec 56, 90p

Chapter 11   An Information Broker

Sue Rugge

Today's information explosion has created a need for a type of service that helps an individual or company untrained in information-gathering techniques to cope with the onslaught of data it faces each day.

Kelly Warnken, *The Information Brokers*, 1982

Sue Rugge's professional career began, quite by accident, in the early seventies in California. She didn't have a chance to go to college, was widowed, and had two children to support. Befriended by her local librarian, she was offered a job as a circulation clerk in the public library. She soon outgrew her clerkship and moved on to fill a vacancy in a division of a General Motor's corporate library, where she quickly learned all she could about library reference services. Within a relatively short period of time, she was answering reference questions for the company's engineers.

Rugge felt comfortable in the corporate library environment even though she was not, as she says, "a trained librarian." One job followed another until she landed at the Friden Company library. But that closed, and she was out on the street again.

Inventing a Niche

"My own sense of economic survival was the driving force to build on what I had learned in my previous jobs," she says. What she did next was to become a landmark decision. It was at this point in 1971 that she met her business partner-to-be, Georgia Finnigan. Together they formed Information Unlimited, which was to be an information-gathering service providing manual and online database research. They each pitched in $125 for letterhead, logos, and a listing in the local Yellow Pages.

Rugge began "cold calling" Silicon Valley electronics firms. She talked to anyone who would listen to her on planes, trains, or taxis and at cocktail parties. "After a while, I found that my friends didn't want to go to parties with me anymore," she says with a grin.

Eventually the phone started ringing asking for research services. By the end of 1972, Information Unlimited supported both partners. By 1978 the company was grossing over $500,000.

But the partnership eventually broke down. Rugge turned right around and formed her own company, Information on Demand, in 1979. By 1982, the company was grossing $1.2 million, serving 15 countries, and employing 37 full-time and 20 part-time workers. The mainstay of the business was document delivery (a beta tester for DIALOG® Information Services new Dialorder document delivery service). Its biggest clients were IBM, 3M, and Bell Labs—all Fortune 100 corporate libraries.

Selling Out to Start Again

In 1982, Pergamon Press, a company owned by British publishing mogul Robert Maxwell, indicated it wanted to buy Information on Demand. By now Rugge was burned out, having worked 12 hours a day every day for most of the past 11 years. Maxwell himself asked Rugge what she wanted for the company. Although he gave her what she asked, Rugge said: "Looking back, I know I should have sold it for more." As part of the deal, she signed a three-year employee contract and a noncompete agreement. In 1987, when her contract was up, Rugge took her money and started a temporary-help service for bed and breakfast inns.

A rather unlikely transition it seemed, and it was somewhat short-lived, because when her noncompete agreement ended in 1987, Rugge was back—this time with yet another company, The Rugge Group, a coalition of independent information consultants grouped together under her marketing umbrella. She had discovered an important niche: She could now provide research expertise in every area of business, legal, medical, and technical research by providing handpicked researchers with superior manual or online research skills and subject expertise. For example, she hired the best patent searcher she could find.

"What if I bring in the business and they do the research?" Rugge thought, because her forté had always been marketing. Most of the other pioneers in the fledgling information brokering business were excellent researchers but less sure of their marketing skills. "You can have all the skill in the world, but if you can't convince someone to use you, then you don't have a business," she observes. She continued to market her research service to Fortune 500 companies as well as many small firms.

Examples of major research projects Rugge and her consultants conducted for clients in the early 1980s:

- Request: For a patent attorney, locate evidence of prior art to challenge a specific patent related to semiconductors.
  This involved hundreds of calls to well-known semiconductor and thermionic industry pioneers to determine if they had ever used or known about a particular concept in the 1960s. It included identifying and locating over 200 industry experts, internationally.
  Total cost for manual and online research: $5,000.
  Result: client was able to break the patent and get his rights back.
- Request: For a plastic container manufacturer, obtain growth figures and identify major trends in all segments of the rigid plastic packaging industry.
  This included extensive interviews with major U.S. competitors, covering conversion rates from glass to plastic, product mix, total sales, technological changes, and the impact of solid waste legislation on industry growth.
  Total cost for manual and online research: $10,000.

Result: being informed about competitors and products, client was able to position their product in the best light.

Requests for smaller projects:

- Request: Generate a list of environmental engineering firms in California with more than 50 employees.
  Cost: $250.

- Request: Determine if a Hong Kong-based company has any U.S. corporate affiliations.
  Cost: $600.

- Request: Identify and get sample copies of all major publications on the travel and tourism industry.
  Cost: $650.

- Request: Search Texas and California newspapers for articles on a particular real estate developer.
  Cost: $300.

Helping to Define an Information-Age Profession

In 1987, Dr. Marilyn Levine, proprietor of an information brokerage in Milwaukee and adjunct faculty at the library school of the University of Wisconsin, organized and led the first meeting to discuss forming an organization of self-employed information entrepreneurs. The 26 attendees at this meeting began to define themselves into what is now called The Association of Independent Information Professionals (AIIP). The original goal of AIIP was threefold:

1. To provide a forum for the discussion of issues and concerns shared by independent information professionals
2. To promote high professional and ethical standards among members
3. To advance knowledge and understanding of the information profession in general and the independent information professional in particular

Also at this meeting, founding members began in earnest to codify and establish professional ethics for information brokers. The Code of Ethical Business Practice for the Association of Independent Professionals was intended to be an important starting point at the first meeting, because it spelled out the importance of professionalism:

Table 11.1   **The Code of Ethical Business Practices for the Association of Independent Information Professionals**

An independent information professional is an information entrepreneur who has demonstrated continuing expertise in the art of finding and organizing information. The independent information professional provides information services on a contractual basis to more than one client. Information professionals serve as objective intermediaries between the client and the information world.

They bear the following responsibilities.

1. To uphold the profession's reputation for honesty, competence, and confidentiality.
2. To give clients the most current and accurate information possible.
3. To help a client understand the sources of information used, and the degree of reliability which can be expected of them.
4. To accept only those projects which are legal and are not detrimental to our profession.
5. To respect client confidentiality.
6. To honor intellectual property rights, and to explain to clients what their obligations may be.
7. To maintain a professional relationship with libraries, and comply with all their rules of access.
8. To assume responsibility for employees' compliance with this code.

Sue Rugge was elected president of AIIP in 1988. Since then, the organization has continued to define itself as integral to the changing information needs of its client base. By 1997 there were over 800 members, and AIIP is now being recognized within the information industry as the voice of the independent information professional. The association works closely with information providers, database vendors, and producers to ensure that the diverse needs of information brokers are considered, while at the same time many producers and vendors of information products have been known to look to AIIP members for direction in the development of their own new products.

The establishment of AIIP was important. "Information gathering is as valid a profession as medicine and bioscience, but has always been looked upon as a stepchild," says Rugge. "Many people think that if they are expert in the subject area, they should be expert in the gathering of information on that subject. For example, one may know how to build a circuit but not necessarily know how to find information about it. If you put an analyst in a spot to do information gathering, then you are not utilizing funds properly; or engineers don't usually know a lot about the Engineering Index (the main tool since 1896 that indexes the engineering literature). They don't talk about gathering but about building."

Information Broker Skills

In addition to information gathering and retrieval, through print and electronic sources, information brokers provide many other information processing or information organization services, many learned through library schools or through extensive experience in the workplace:

- Cataloging print and electronic resources
- Competitive intelligence
- Clipping services
- Database design and development
- Digital library development
- Document delivery
- Education/seminars/training in information literacy
- Indexing and abstracting
- Market analysis and industry services
- Public records research
- Thesaurus building

Although many information brokers are generalists, many also have diverse subject expertise in such business areas as advertising, marketing, demographics, insurance, and international trade, and in technical areas such as aerospace, agriculture, biosciences, chemicals, engineering, environment, food, genealogy, health care, information technology, litigation research, pharmaceuticals, technology transfer, and patents and trademarks.

Burned Out

On October 20, 1991, Sue Rugge's world fell apart. Upon returning to her home in Oakland from a business trip, she was greeted at the airport by the news that her home had burned to the ground in the Oakland-

Berkeley Hills fires. In her home was her business and all of her records, which were destroyed.

Shortly thereafter, a message went out to Section Zero, a bulletin board on CompuServe for AIIP members:

> A Heartfelt Thanks
> from Sue Rugge (76220, 454)
> I want to thank all of you in Section Zero for your immediate and continuous outpouring of notes, calls, and cash. Once again, the generosity, camaraderie, and caring that is so unique to our industry has evidenced itself. I am both humbled and proud to be a member of AIIP.
> Next to my garden—which I hope will grow again someday—music brings me the most pleasure. To receive the hand-picked recordings complete with handmade covers and the hardware on which to play it was fantastic, to hear the beautiful arias of Puccini and Verdi enabled my husband Hank and I to believe that our world could be put back together...When you lose everything—business, home, and personal effects—you are immediately reminded of what is most important—PEOPLE. Thank you all from the bottom of my heart for being there when I needed it most.

Rising from the Ashes

Within a year and a half, Rugge's home was rebuilt on the same spot where it had stood and she had started yet another company, the Information Professionals Institute (IPI), in partnership with information broker Helen Burwell, information consultant, a past president of AIIP, and publisher of the annual *Burwell World Directory of Information Brokers*.[1] In the meantime, she sold the rights to use her company name, The Rugge Group, and it eventually became a division of Teltech, which offers primary and secondary research services in a variety of fields.

The Information Mentoring Niche

Another niche was invented: "If you are too old to do it, you can teach it," said Rugge. And so she and her partner Burwell began providing seminars for the continuing education of information professionals and would-be information brokers through The Information Professionals Institute. The seminars are presented frequently (with some variation in programs) across the United States, often in conjunction with information content-oriented conferences such as National Online, Online World, the Society of Competitive Intelligence Professionals, and the Special Libraries Association.

Seminars provide the business, legal, and technical considerations for starting an information brokering business. There are also several specialty seminars offered relating to public records, online searching, and competitor intelligence. With a click to http://www.ipn.net/ipi, you can gain access to the Information Professionals Institute homepage, where Rugge and Burwell have set up a one-stop shop for software, training, and books by and for information professionals.

Choosing from the Heart

In 1992, Rugge wrote a book in conjunction with PC telecommunications expert Alfred Glossbrenner. *The Information Broker's Handbook*[2] became a definitive work on information brokering, and by 1995 the second edition was released. (A third edition is now available.) In it, Rugge discusses the pros and cons of becoming an information broker and she is honestly blunt: "If there's anything else you can do for a living that meets your own personal goals, by all means do it. You will never be able to make a rational, cost-justified case for choosing this profession. The choice has to come from the heart." Why does she say this? Because she wants to immediately clear away any misconceptions would-be information brokers might have about hanging out a shingle and getting rich overnight.

Selling Expertise, Not Information

Rugge explains to those who call for information about her seminars that information brokering is not a business limited to people with masters of library science degrees, but it does require expertise for finding and analyzing information, an ability to operate a small business and market a service, and a basic affinity with computers and telecommunications. "These skills and abilities can be learned," she says.

She is quick to say in her seminar that the reason many information brokers fail is because of their inability to sell a nebulous service. She also points out that brokers sell their expertise in knowing how to gather information, not the information itself. And because they are selling their time, they have to charge even if they don't find the information they are looking for.

> There is no little black box to sell. Clients don't want to pay for something they can't touch or see. The Industrial Revolution concept of replication does not apply here. Each time the phone rings, we are starting over—the same question is not asked twice. In fact, most companies and people are extremely reluctant to part with their dollars, and they simply find a way to do without. Many are successful enough to get by. The fact that they might have done even better and had even greater success if they had used the services of an information professional is difficult to prove. We know it's true. We know that day in and day out, the company or concern that has the best information has more potential to out-perform the one that is merely "getting by." But often in this era of mediocrity, "getting by" is more than sufficient.

In *The Information Broker's Handbook*, Rugge emphasizes her point about paying for information broker's services:

> ...the demand for information is limitless. There is hardly anyone who wouldn't like to know more about a topic of personal, professional, or business interest. People will be glad to accept anything you can provide...But don't ask them to pay for it.[3]

She also explains why there is resistance to paying for information and information services:

> The concept of information gathering, which is usually associated with a librarian, suffers from what we call the "Carnegie syndrome." It is the idea that somehow all information should be free.[4]

Rugge notes that information brokering takes place in a very different working environment than the more secure library system. "If you are an information broker, everything is on the line, both personally and financially. If you're promising things you can't deliver, you are probably not going to get paid."

The Six Crucial Elements of
Information Brokering

What Rugge points out in her seminars, her publications, and her conversations with would-be information brokers is that they must have certain "core competencies" to be successful. These six crucial elements are: intelligence, personality, education, background, training, and skills. Brains and personality are the most critical, she claims. By intelligence, she means being clever and creative, "because there are no instruction manuals to show you how to solve specific problems in this field." She also mentions that an information broker must be a quick study, be able to assimilate, make sense of large numbers of facts quickly, provide excellent recall, and adapt quickly.

When she looked for employees, she found it hard to find people with the right combination of personality and innate ability. Rugge points out that like many computer programmers, people who are good at information often aren't good at relating to people. "What is necessary to be an information broker is someone who is great with information but also with clients, i.e., who can draw out what the client really needs and then decide what can be done to help them," she says.

Rugge believes that brokers must also be educators. "When we go to market our services, we must educate before we can sell. I don't think most executives know how to answer questions about their information needs, because they don't think in those terms." She suggests that it may be up to information providers to show end users ways to verbalize and recognize their own information needs.

When asked about what else one should look for in a good information broker, she says: "Self-confidence. If you don't have confidence in your own credibility, then you can't sell it. But the most important skill is communication. You are projecting your profession and your credibility, and it is your responsibility to walk down the decision path with clients and ask what kind of data they need to make this decision."

One of her first questions to a client is: "What are you trying to accomplish?" It is only then that she can ascertain how she can help. She also learns "from talking, even just chatting on a regular basis, calling them up when you haven't talked to them for a month and saying,

'What's new, what are you working on these days?'" Then her imagination comes into play, and her response might be: "Given what you have said to me, do you think that looking at someone's background or what the *Wall Street Journal* has said about this industry in the last year would be helpful in making your decision?"

Rugge says that "realistically, information brokering is hard work. It's rewarding, intellectually, emotionally, and sometimes financially, but extremely labor intensive. Our biggest challenge is ignorance on the executives' part as to the resources that are available, and it is our job to help them learn what we can get for them that will make their work easier."

Hanging Around the Water Cooler

Sue Rugge meets all the criteria for being a good information broker. She is a quick study and an excellent communicator, always making an effort to keep lines of communication open to facilitate exchange so that she can make connections for her clients between the information and the application. Rugge says of her early days at Friden: "I used to hang around the water cooler with the guys, finding out what information they needed."

Where will you find her these days? You can still sign up for her information broker seminars, and you will most likely see her stop in at one of the booths set up at information conferences, where she guides would-be brokers. Or you can find her at the electronic water cooler now located on the AIIP listserve on the Internet at AIIP-L@hp.ipnetwork.com. For information on how to become a member or subscribe to the listserve, go to the AIIP Homepage, http://www.aiip.org, or check in at the Information Professionals Institute homepage on the Web at: http://www.ipn.net/ipi.

Roaming the Hills of Tuscany

Rugge's most recent enterprise is Italian villas, and you can find her roaming the hills of Tuscany looking for properties to rent for her new company, Italia Reservations, now a booming business. She will tell you she is winding down from the turbulent days of information brokering, now learning to enjoy her new home and garden and traveling with her husband. But knowing Rugge, whatever she does, personally or professionally, it comes from the heart.

Notes

1.   Helen Burwell, *The Burwell World Directory of Information Brokers* (Houston, TX: Burwell Enterprises, 1997-1998).
2.   Sue Rugge and Alfred Glossbrenner, *The Information Broker's Handbook*, 2nd ed. (New York: Windcrest/McGraw-Hill, 1995).
3.   Ibid, 60.
4.   Ibid, 7.

For More Information

I.   Resources available for, by, and about information brokers:

- The Information Professionals Institute
  46 Hiller Drive
  Oakland, CA 94618
  510-649-9743
  http://www.ipn.net/ipi
  E-mail: 76220.454@CompuServe.com
- The Association of Independent Information Professionals (AIIP)
  234 W. Delaware Ave.
  Pennington, NJ 08534
  Voice: 609-730-8759
  Fax: 609-730-8469
  WWW address: http://www.aiip.org/
- *The Burwell World Directory of Information Brokers*
  Helen Burwell
  Burwell Enterprises
  3724 FM 1960 West, Suite 214
  Houston, Texas 77068
  http://ipn.net/ipi/worlddir.html

II.   In their own words...what information brokers do.

Following is a brief summary of recent information broker projects
that illustrate the diversity and variety of their services: (please note
fees are only guidelines)

Name of Information Broker: Paula Eiblum (Infocus Research
Services, Rockville, MD)
Description of Project: Our company was asked to compile a list
of reference materials on detailed road transportation statistics for 12
major cities in the Far East and South America. The scope and
generous budget of the project allowed for online and manual
research, as well as for purchasing books and documents from the
sources.
Resources Used: Our research staff used the following resources
from an overview to identify contracts and experts in the field:
- Gale's *Encyclopedia of Associations*
- DIALOG® Information Services/Knight Ridder databases
- United Nations publications catalogs
- *Books in Print*
- Library of Congress online catalog
- Transportation library online catalogs in Texas, California,
  Michigan
- Internet resources and transportation megasites

Outcome: After identifying reference materials that were common
to the major transportation libraries searched, we interviewed the
librarians at these institutions and asked for their expert opinion
regarding the materials, specifically related to statistics for the cities
in our project. We compiled a list of all reference materials that were
common to several of the libraries we had searched, indicating
books, journals, and conference proceedings. We contacted
associations in the United States and abroad to further confirm the
validity and timeliness of the choices. We identified the world's
leading expert on transportation statistics and contacted him overseas. He sent us many of his papers and confirmed to us that our
research was as comprehensive and exhaustive as possible. We then
purchased three major reference books from publishers in the United
States, United Kingdom, and Switzerland. In addition to providing
books and a list of print materials, we searched Internet sites for
specific cities and provided all materials that were relevant to the

client's needs. We provided the client with the name of the expert for future consultation.

Fee: The budget for the project was $2,000, including the materials. The books cost approximately $600. A total of $1,800 was billed.

Name of Information Broker: Chris Dobson (F1 Services, Dallas, Texas)

Description of Project: A Fortune 100 company had just closed its one-person corporate library and wanted to establish a virtual library for employees at the corporate headquarters. We were asked to duplicate, with online or CD-ROM products, the material in the print collection and identify the few unique items that could not be obtained in electronic form. We were to provide a solution within two months, using stand-alone equipment to facilitate rapid deployment of the system.

Resources Used: The first step was to conduct an information audit. We surveyed headquarters' employees and followed up with interviews of key individuals and frequent library users to determine precisely which resources were needed. Our staff already had extensive knowledge both of our client's industry and of available online services. We partnered with vendors of online and CD-ROM products to further leverage our skills. We used online services and the Internet to further research the products we considered.

Outcome: After compiling data from the survey and interviews, we could easily identify the type of information needed to conduct company business. We examined the material in the print collection and selected those books needed to facilitate decision making, which fit on one book truck. Most print materials were general management texts rather than critical industry publications. All other information was available in electronic form. Next, we obtained demos or trials of the potential services. Many were overlapping or presented similar information. In addition to content, we rated the user interface for ease of use by novice searchers. Format was also an important consideration. All the services we ultimately selected were available through the Internet, facilitating expansion of services to users' desktops. These services also accommodate multiple passwords for charging back to the user departments. Finally, cost was a determinant. All our vendor partners were willing to negotiate a contract that took into account the initial learning curve the company would experience as the new virtual library was introduced. We arranged a meeting with corporate decision makers and our vendor partners to present our plan and demonstrate the selected products. We recommended to the vendors the searches that would best highlight the unique qualities of each product. In addition to recommendations for services, our final report contained equipment and software specifications, layout, and furnishings for a centralized location for the stand-alone equipment and materials, recommended print monograph and serial publications, a list of relevant World Wide Web sites, and the estimated cost of both establishing and maintaining the virtual library.

Fee: The all-inclusive fee for this project was $15,000

Name of Information Broker: Susan M. Detweiler (The Detweiler Group, Ft. Wayne, Indiana)
Description of Project: We periodically write overviews of particular medical supply or device markets, for example, gloves, wound closures, and dental and surgical instruments. The glove market project is typical: Research and write an overview of the market, including size, history, projections, rankings of major players, and the environmental parameters of the supply of latex.
Resources Used: Sources include the usual medical industry trade magazines, investment reports, Securities & Exchange Commission (SEC) submissions (primarily 10-k's), business magazine and newspaper press, sources, online, and telephone calls to the Malaysian Rubber Institute, OSHA, the American Dental Association, and other organizations.
Fee: $3,000 to $5,000 depending on the time involved and the resources available.

Name of Information Broker: Lynn Peterson (PFC Information Services, Oakland, California)
Description of Project: We were contacted by an attorney who requested that we conduct a search of the public records on file for an individual who was running an "investment club" for senior citizens. The attorney had been contacted by the adult children of a retired gentleman who had made a $20,000 investment and was

about to invest another $20,000. The return on the $20,000 was to
be at least $500,000, all within approximately 160 days. The
children were alarmed because the situation sounded too good to be
true.

We were given a budget of $750 and were told that the information
was needed by the end of the day, as the father was going to another
meeting of the investment club that evening.

Resources and Methodology: The only information our client
could provide regarding the subject was his name and his company's
name. We had no address information, date of birth, or social
security number. We were fortunate that the subject's name was
relatively uncommon and that the geographic area to be searched
was California, where the availability of online data is good.

We started by searching DBT (Database Technologies, Inc.) for
records of the subject's address history, social security number, and
date of birth. We also ran a credit header and found that the
employment listed was as a real estate broker. This preliminary
research was essential, as we needed to know where to search for
records and we needed identifying data to determine whether the
records found were relevant to the subject, or to other individuals
with the same name.

CDB Infotek was utilized to research civil litigation, criminal
records, real property, and bankruptcy, liens, and judgments. We
found numerous state and federal tax liens. We also found that the
subject had been sued repeatedly, that there were several unpaid
judgments against him, and that he had declared bankruptcy.
Although the subject had formerly owned real property in
California, the properties were in foreclosure. We also found several
corporations in California and Nevada for which the subject was
listed as president and/or registered agent. All of the companies
found had been suspended for failure to pay franchise tax.

Since the subject's credit header indicated that he had been
employed as a real estate broker, we called the California
Department of Real Estate and found that his license had been
revoked for violation of the California Business and Professions
Code. We also utilized PACER (Public Access to Court Electronic
Records) to search for cases from the U.S. District Courts of
California and found a conviction for "Conspiracy to Convert to

Own Use a Veterans Administration Guaranteed Loan on Residential Property."

Outcome: If we had had more time we would have conducted on-site research in several jurisdictions for which criminal and civil court records were not available online. However, the public records we uncovered were sufficient to prevent any further investments from being made. Our client planned to refer the matter to the district attorney.

Fee: $750.

Name of Information Broker: Dr. Martin Goffman (Martin Goffman Associates, Edison, New Jersey)

Why use a specialty searcher?

Patent searching is a specialty. Although many search professionals do examine the patent literature on behalf of clients, this is one specialty area where it is necessary to know the nuances of the patent writings themselves.

Permit me to cite one simple example. You conduct a patent novelty search, and uncover four references. However, these represent only some of the features that your corporate client requested. Your client then proceeds to file a patent application based on the results of your search, spending $10,000 for preparation and prosecution of the application. Three days later, his application is rejected—the patent examiner found a "102 knockout" (35 U.S.C. 102) patent reference, more commonly known as a prior art reference. The examiner knew where to look and manually searched the right subclass until identifying a drawing that described the client's invention. You, of course, missed the drawings with your online search!

In another search, perhaps you did not find the damning reference because your search strategy included a metal oxide and "substrate," but the reference disclosed a "wafer" that is equivalent to the substrate. Thus instead of appearing in the electronic components class and subclasses that you searched, the knockout reference was categorized in a chemical processes subclass. The knockout may even have antedated the online database that you searched...So easy to miss; so difficult to find!

To successfully conduct a novelty search, you must be absolutely familiar with the general scientific discipline that pertains to the invention. You must understand the invention and be aware of the terms of art used in the field. You must know the patent process, how the patent literature is organized, and how to access this literature.

If you cannot do a professional job, you should find a professional who can. *Ignorance* discredits your own abilities and costs you in the long run. *Expertise* brings your client success, and you will reap the benefits of repeat business and referrals.

Name of Information Broker: Stephanie Ardito (Ardito Information & Research, Wilmington, Delaware)

Description of Project: Copyright training project

Project Summary: Ardito Information & Research, Inc. was contacted by a nonprofit association to: (1) provide an audit of the organization's photocopying and online reproduction practices; (2) advise about copyright compliance, including protection of the organization's original materials (newsletters, magazines, Web site), and mechanisms that would permit duplication of other publishers' materials; and (3) furnish training to the staff about the importance of honoring intellectual property rights.

Project Resources Used: One day was scheduled for on-site meetings with various association staff to review printed and electronic materials being copied for internal and external distribution, and with library staff to assess online searching and downloading practices. To counsel the association about copyright compliance, the Copyright Act of 1976 was downloaded from the Internet, relevant sections were highlighted, and recommendations about duplicating copyrighted materials were made. In addition, the Copyright Clearance Center was contacted for information on its services that would allow reproduction of materials in exchange for royalty payments to registered publishers.

An online search of commercial databases and various Internet sites listing copyright resources was conducted; relevant articles, litigated court case decisions of direct relevance to the association, and Internet URLs addressing photocopying practices (i.e., educational and/or personal use versus commercial use) were identified and provided.

Three two-hour training sessions were conducted for association staff following the audit and after the association's attorneys had reviewed our firm's recommendations and implemented association copyright policies. The training sessions reviewed the history of copyright, the Copyright Act of 1976 and its 1978 revisions (including author's rights, the duration of copyright, and public domain works that are not protected by copyright laws), and fair use versus commercial use of copyrighted materials.

Project Outcome: The association had placed itself at great risk for lawsuits, as hundreds of illegal copies were being made for the membership each year. The organization registered with the Copyright Clearance Center to pay publishers for photocopies, displayed signs over every photocopier to remind employees about the legality of reproducing copyrighted materials, reviewed all internal documents and Web sites for copyright statements to protect the association's original works, and started a membership awareness program.

Fee: $3,000: $1,000 for the audit; $1,000 to research the copyright literature and prepare a report of recommendations; $1,000 for three two-hour training sessions.

Chapter 12   A Director of Research

Allan E. Rypka

> The information you don't know may or may not be harmful but what
> you do know that is not true is lethal.

Ret. Admiral John Butts
Director of Naval Intelligence, spoken in 1983

Allan E. Rypka knows a lot about how people are becoming more proficient in the abuse of technology and information. When asked to comment on the subject of information warfare, he says, "It is far better to be well informed than well armed. There is always someone out there who is better armed."

Rypka's own knowledge base is multidisciplinary, with two master's degrees from the Naval Post Graduate School (one in intelligence and one in strategic planning) and a degree from the Defense Intelligence College and the Monterey Aviation Safety Management Program.

With this background, Rypka has become proficient in technology, intelligence collecting, analysis, and the management of high-level research projects. For a number of years, he worked in a Fortune 50 company (TRW), analyzing communication and navigation systems. More recently he started his own company, Focused Research International (FRI), which provides a service he describes as "Information Age research support for government and industry, which is both a user and generator of information." Areas of specialization for Rypka and his staff are intelligence, law enforcement, telecommunications, modeling and simulation, and aviation. Clients include the Department of Defense, state and local law enforcement, Fortune 100 firms, and small businesses.

Allan Rypka describes himself as a "meta-user" of information about information resources, and an "information provider or intermediary" for delivering information to his clients to keep them informed of current developments. He keeps one foot in the user area and one in the provider area.

The "Total Knowledge of Mankind" Theory

When Rypka talks about keeping up with new (and old) knowledge he mentions his "Total Knowledge of Mankind" theory. It is his own graphical version of the "information explosion," and it provides an illustration of how all fields of knowledge are expanding. The theory was developed following a project for one of Rypka's clients, an educator, who asked him to help identify the growth of information sources in her very specialized subject area by going back 30 years in the literature and moving forward to now. "The client was considered an authority in her area, a visionary," says Rypka. "Based on our own research, she discovered she had not heard of 85 out of 100 of the authors identified in the available electronic citations!"

Rypka admits that his theory is partly opinion and partly subjective, that the definitions of information and knowledge can be confusing, and that no one can really get a grasp of the growth at this point because things are moving too fast. His theory goes something like this:

> In 1500 B.C., given all the knowledge in the world in all fields, it took 3000 years for the knowledge to double, (i.e., by the Renaissance). It then took only 400 years to double again, (i.e., by the Industrial Revolution). And now, it is doubling every six to eight months in every field.

Figure 12.1 The Total Knowledge of Mankind

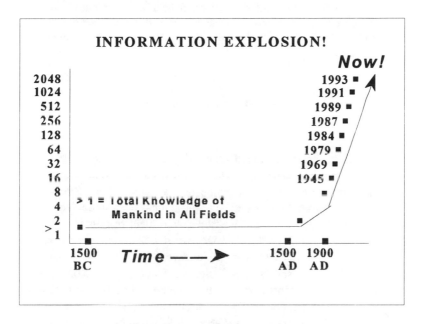

How Rypka Lives with
Information Overload

Rypka says that in our current higher education system (where knowledge is generally produced), Ph.D.s often can't or don't keep up with the total breadth of basics in their field because they are too narrowly focused. "Now, *nobody* can keep up in their field," he says. Rypka cites an eye doctor he knows who keeps up with changes in his field by forming network circles of specialists. He says that he calls his circles to ask "What's new? Of course the typical businessperson can't call competitors and ask 'what's new.'" So where is he/she going to find the critical information? Rypka says:

> It's not going to be getting any better. It's not just the amount of information that exists, it's the ability to move it around, merge it with other information, analyze it, create new knowledge, and employ it in the missions or goals of the individual or company. The only

way to survive within this explosion of information for the individual, business, law enforcement, or whatever field, in my opinion, is to swim in it, i.e., to do constant research in areas that might be brought to bear. The problems we see today are just the nub of what's going to happen.

Rypka's Own Knowledge Base of Technical Information Warfare

Rypka is always armed with statistics, reports, and anecdotes of his knowledge and experiences in what is known as technical information warfare, considered high-tech crime and an area where Rypka says "business is booming" for criminals because it has been so neglected. For example, Rypka cites an unclassified government resource, *The Electronic Intrusion Threat to National Security and Emergency Preparedness Telecommunications*,[1] which is "loaded with historical, technical and estimative data" that shows information warfare capabilities observed in 30 countries. The report says that the concern domestically is that the Public Switched Network (PSN) is threatened by electronic intruders. Possible effects of threats to the PSN include denial or disruption of service, unauthorized monitoring or disclosure of sensitive information, unauthorized modification of network databases/services, and fraud/ financial loss. Each effect may disrupt or degrade national security and emergency preparedness (NS/EP) telecommunications, which are provided by commercial carriers.

Anecdotal recounting of Rypka's experiences can make one feel very uneasy about the enormous potential of threats to our daily technology processes. Rypka says that these high-tech crimes can affect anyone and everyone. "It can happen in any jurisdiction that has banks, ATM machines, or telephones," and "yes" says Rypka, "your calls to order a T-shirt from Land's End can be monitored and your credit card can be sabotaged. Preventing abuse through and on the Internet will require individuals to be alert at all times."

Rypka says that these issues are now being recognized, programs developed, and policy changes being made. The Federal Communications Commission (FCC) and other agencies are now struggling with how to proceed. He notes that his company (FRI) participated in a national project, The Public Safety Wireless Advisory Committee[2] (http://www.pswac.ntia.doc.gov) whose final report will be provided by the FCC to congressional committees drafting legislation for the Information Age. For more information on recent telecommunications legislation, Rypka recommends going to the FCC homepage at http://www.fcc.gov or to the Commerce Department at http://www.doc.gov. For a copy of the Telecommunications Act of 1996 and the Communications Decency Act Rypka recommends: http:/www.state.wi.us/agencies/dpi/www/telecom_act.html.

Assessing Law Enforcement Technical Capabilities: Using 1970s Technologies and Working in 17th Century Buildings

Rypka talks of a subcategory of technical information warfare, law enforcement technology:

> Only five percent of law enforcement agencies in the U.S. are federal. That leaves approximately 17,000 police departments in state and local municipalities across the U.S. to fight crime that includes murder, rape, robbery, burglary, drug trafficking, theft, assault, weapons offenses, and driving offenses.

Rypka says that in big cities there is a "high-tech veneer" for fighting basic crimes and felonies, but not for smaller state and local agencies, for which FRI is particularly suited to provide low-cost, hi-tech assistance. "Often the most sophisticated technology available to many law enforcement agents is voice radio," says Rypka. He mentions the sheriff's building where he once consulted: "It is still standing, built in the seventeenth century."

Rypka's own research into law enforcement technology is abundant, with real-life stories of proliferating crimes that go unpunished because of lack of funding, basic computer illiteracy within crime units, noninteroperability of radios where it is difficult or impossible to communicate because of different radio frequencies (UHF/VHF), incompatibility between old and new systems, radio interference, maintenance of older systems, and too few phones. Rypka cites one police chief who said, "We are a busy signal away from disaster all the time."

A law enforcement and communication needs assessment conducted by Rypka on behalf of a state and local police client revealed:

> Only 20 percent had access to a fax machines; they had limited knowledge of how to develop a strategic technology plan with a view to integrate and/or bypass technologies they didn't need; there were only a few units at about the level of technology of a small business, i.e., they had e-mail and a fax, but not necessarily integrated, and they certainly didn't have voice mail, e-mail, and fax integrated like some of the bigger businesses do.

Overall assessments of technical capabilities of several state and local police clients led Rypka to these conclusions:

> All were tight on funds and most of the funds they did get were spent on personnel and vehicles; there were usually no funds for information and analysis support; there was very little knowledge about new technologies that could make a difference in the way crime should be fought in this country. And without new technology, there was no adequate access to critical information needed to operate, or to compete with criminals.

Providing Solutions and Recommendations: New Technologies and Better Use of Information Resources

Rypka's research and analysis helped one of the jurisdictions better articulate, identify, and understand its current and potential problems. It also provided a number of solutions as well as recommendations for avoiding future problems and saving money. Rypka believes that developing an infrastructure within the agency for information and analysis support is a critical component of intelligent crime prevention and law enforcement. Thus in one case a range of information products were developed to help the client answer important questions such as "which uniform manufacturers could utilize CAD (computer-automated design) technology?" The result? By being able to identify and contact manufacturers, the agency could then find more cost-effective, instantaneous, precision-fitted replacements. Or in another case, "What options were available to replace existing radio capabilities (ear/speaker/ microphone assembly)?" The result? By identifying the options and analyzing the information, the anticipated cost by the agency of buying new portable radios at $150,000 was found to be less than $8,000.

Rypka also compiled a list for law enforcement agents interested in learning more about electronic information resources in their own areas of knowledge. The list, "Law Enforcement Technology Information Sources and Research Assistance," describes commercial online databases, CD-ROM resources, government sources and agencies, bulletin boards, Internet sources, and information specialists/brokers lists. "For example," says Rypka, "they learned that the Bureau of Prisons has a Bulletin Board still in existence (1-202-307-3104) and now a homepage at http://www.bop.gov/ that provides an overview of Bureau of Prisons programs and software, and the National Criminal Justice Reference Service (NCJRS), 301-251-5269 or http://www.ncjrs.org/homepage.htm contains current news, announcements, and online publications about crime. "This law enforcement list we compiled," Rypka says, "eventually became part of a larger project done for a National Institute of Justice grant."

The Need for New Educational Constructs

One issue that came to Rypka's attention while putting together the list of electronic information resources for law enforcement agencies was the near total lack of serious thinking about training law enforcement agents to use these resources. Most attention has been paid to teaching basic computer literacy for information processing. Issues about how to find information, to interpret the new tools of the trade, such as graphical and mapping images, or to analyze investigative reports are not considered.

Although Rypka dislikes using the word "paradigm" because it is overworked, he says that there is a need for a new information skills paradigm that combines research with analysis. "This new 'educational construct' (paradigm) should be able to provide businesses (and military) with employees who can do custom research while relating it to the operating needs of the client." In addition, he explains that a new "educational construct" would provide businesses with a work force with the ability to analyze new knowledge. He suggests that the new construct be able to "combine the skills of high school (for finding information), a B.A./M.A. (for putting it together and analyzing), and a Ph.D. (for creating new knowledge)." Rypka remembers his final exam in Aviation Safety Management school where he was given a pile of junk to analyze, identify the cause of the mishap, and outline actions needed to prevent a recurrence. He calls it "a real-world multidisciplinary application," that all businesses and local governments should develop.

Moving Toward a National Intelligence Strategy

At about the same time Rypka was working with law enforcement agency issues, there was a growing concern in U.S. Military Intelligence (MI) and in companies, large and small, that the United States was losing its competitive edge to other countries, and that organization and access to information were important parts of this competitive edge. The thinking and reading in intelligence circles current at that time, he notes, was about the "mother lode" of information and research becoming available on the Internet and residing in commercial and government repositories.

This growing interest by the military in intelligence sources resulted in a new directive on Open Source Intelligence (OSINT) that is now considered a new identifiable source of information for intelligence use, i.e., raw intelligence (of which the vast majority comes from published, usually recorded sources), as distinct from other categories of sources of military intelligence such as HUMINT (Human Intelligence), SIGINT (Signals Intelligence), or IMINT (Imagery Intelligence, which some refer to as "the clandestine collection" of the world of intelligence).

The final draft for the OSINT directive was issued on 1 November 1994 as the Director of Central Intelligence Directive (DCID). The definitive text in the field of OSINT is called "Open Source Intelligence Resources for the Military Intelligence Officer," written in 1993.[3] This directive and the OSINT text were significant because they essentially provided a "new order of march" for military intelligence that a more organized and focused effort must be made to take full advantage of open source materials, defined as Open Source Information (OSI) that includes:

> Publicly available information (i.e., any member of the public could lawfully obtain the information by request or observation), as well as other unclassified information that has limited public distribution or access. Open source information also includes any information that may be used in an unclassified context without compromising national security or intelligence sources and methods. If the information is not publicly available, certain legal requirements relating to collection, retention, and dissemination may apply.[4]

The report included an important subset of open source intelligence called gray literature, defined as:

> Gray literature, regardless of media, can include, but is not limited to, research reports, technical reports, economic reports, trip reports, working papers, discussion papers, unofficial government documents, proceedings, preprints, research reports, studies, dissertations and theses, trade literature, market surveys, and newsletters. This material cuts across scientific, political, socioeconomic, and military disciplines.[5]

The report also lists the Internet (at the time relatively unknown as military intelligence) as a subset of open source intelligence.

Rypka reports that his company was recognized by the Department of Defense as the first information brokerage to participate in real-world contingency planning as a result of FRI's efforts to gather open source information on the Internet in support of military planning for Bosnian incursion. His firm gathered thousands of files, images, and TV and radio broadcasts from the Internet while simultaneously developing training materials to aid government analysts in gathering similar data. The resulting database and training materials have served throughout the NATO I-FOR (Incursion Force) presence in Bosnia.

Since the OSINT directives, information now available on the Internet has continued its explosive growth. If fact, if you were to connect to the Internet, you would find that there are now links to hundreds of government agencies worldwide concerned with the issues of missile and space intelligence, ground intelligence, medical intelligence, naval intelligence, information warfare, systems security, and productivity. Here are just a few:

- Foreign Broadcast Information Service
- National Security Agency
- U.S. Air Force, Air Intelligence Agency
- National Air Intelligence
- U.S. Armed Forces Medical Intelligence
- U.S. Army, Training and Doctrine Command
- U.S. Army, National Ground Intelligence
- U.S. Central Intelligence Agency
- U.S. Defense Intelligence Agency
- U.S. Federal Bureau of Investigation
- U.S. Marine Corps Intelligence
- U.S. Navy, Office of Naval Intelligence

Rypka first heard of the Internet effort (then called ARPA-NET) in 1972. In 1979, Rypka used the Internet for the first time but did not find it user friendly or a productive use of his time. It was during the Iran hostage crisis that he became involved and is now an active user of the Internet for reviewing government resources and keeping his clients informed of current developments, and his information gathering and usage is evolving with the growth of resources on the Internet. In addition to those listed above, Rypka mentions a few (but not all) of the Internet resources he currently uses to keep up and to stay ahead:

- Primary list servers (for communications with other information brokers and subject specialists)
- AIIP (Association of Independent Information Professionals): aiip-1@hp.ipnetwork.com
- Open Source Professionals List: ospro@pscusa.com
- Telecom Cities: listproc@list.nyu.edu
- C4I (Command, Control, Communications, Computers and Intelligence Branch of the U.S. Navy): C4I-pro@azure.stl. nps.navy.mil
- Infopro List (private list for licensed private investigators, investigative reporters and information brokers): infopro@hp. ipnetwork.com
- Primary list mailers (for receiving information about the changes in the Internet in areas of most concern for Rypka's clients)

- InterNic (Net Happenings): listserv@internic.net
- Enlow News: majordomo@twins.cftnet.com
- Net Announce: nalist@erspros.com
- Tip World: tips@tipworld.com
- Techno Times: techknow@technotimes.com

Rypka also provides the names of important intelligence and government resources (available to all) on the World Wide Web:

Intelligence links:

- 2600 Magazine ("The Hacker's Quarterly")
  http://www.2600.com
- 434th Military Intelligence Detachment (Strategic)
  http://www.eajardines.com/434mid.html
- Central Intelligence Agency
  http://www.odci.gov/cia
- Declassified Satellite Photographs
  http://edcwww.cr.usgs.gov/dclass/dclass.html
- Encryption Policy Resource Page
  http://www.crypto.com
- HotWired and Wired Privacy Archive—Fight for Your Right to Electronic Privacy!
  http://www.hotwired.com/clipper/index
- Intelligence Links
  http://csi.preby.edu/~jquinton/intel.html
- The Open Source Quarterly
  http://www.eajardines.com/osq.html
- Virtual World of Spies and Intelligence
  http://www.dreamscape.com/frankvad/covert.html
- Welcome to Open Source Solutions, Inc.
  http://www.oss.net/oss

Government links:

- FedWorld: http://www.fedworld.com
- Centers for Disease Control and Prevention: http://www.cdc/gov/
- FEDERAL NEWS SERVICE: http://www.fnsq.com/
- Library of Congress homepage (links to Intelligence): http://www.loc.gov/
- State and Local Governments on the Net: http://www.piperinfo.com/state/states.html

- Council of State Governments: http://www.csg.org
- U.S. Department of Commerce: http://www.doc.gov

Industrial Espionage Concerns

With the growth of the Internet and more recognition of information resources in the military and in business, other issues of concern are developing. Rypka especially notes the Economic Espionage Act of 1996, initiated in the Computer Crime and Intellectual Property Section, Criminal Division, U.S. Justice Department, and the FBI's ANSIR Program, regarding the acquisition of "trade secrets"—including production processes, bid estimates, and production schedules—which will now result in federal penalties, including fines, forfeiture, and imprisonment.

New Turf Issues

Another new area Rypka is now "swimming in" is security in information searching. He provides an example from a recent article from *Computerworld* entitled "Computer Security Is Not Protection, It's Delay":

> Conducting a security audit of 15,000 Pentagon systems in which vulnerabilities had previously been pointed out to systems managers for correction, the Information Warfare Division of the Defense Information Agency found that it was able to gain access to almost nine out of ten of the systems simply by using publicly available techniques. A top agency administrator says that security managers need to focus less on preventing outside penetration and more on detecting intrusions and reacting with immediate shutdowns. "You have to view security as buying you time. It's not protection. It's delay."[6]

Rypka comments:

> Up to now all money has been spent on system intrusion and how to keep intruders out of your system. What we are concerned

with is detecting versus preventing intrusion. We are looking at security of information searching where others can see what information you are looking for, thus learning your secrets and your information needs.

This area is referred to in the intelligence world as OPSEC (operations security). "In industry," Rypka explains, "this means secure competitive intelligence efforts. For government, it means protecting the 'collection requirements' of intelligence agencies, whether national security or local law enforcement."

"Research is needed in this area, particularly on the utility of 'anonymisers' that remove elements of your own cyber-identity and provide you with an anonymous identity," says Rypka. "At this stage of development, we think it is better to focus on the rats, rather than to invent a better mousetrap."

Rypka refers to an important reference resource that calls for more research in this area. It is the "Testimony to Congress at a House Technology Committee" by Gene Safford in 1997, which says that "there are only four academic institutions in the U.S. with dedicated computer security research laboratories. Of the 5,000 Ph.D.s in computer science in the last five years, only 16 came from those four security programs and only eight were U.S. citizens."

Rypka's previous work in this evolving specialty gives his company the distinction of being the first information brokerage to develop and implement an OPSEC plan during research for a government client. He believes his company has now accumulated a significant and strategic knowledge base to help define these issues of critical security and to make recommendations to find important solutions.

We hope you will Allan—time is of the essence!

Notes

1.   *The Electronic Intrusion Threat to National Security and Emergency Preparedness Telecommunications*, National Communication System, 701 South Courthouse Road, Arlington, VA 22204-2198, December 1994.

2.   Final Report of the Public Safety Wireless Advisory Committee to the Federal Communications Commission, Reed E. Hundt, Chairman and The National Telecommunications and Information Administrations, Larry Irving,

Assistant Secretary of Commerce for Communications and Information, 11 September 1996.

3.   *The Open Source Intelligence Resources for the Military Intelligence Officer,* Second Edition, 434th Military Intelligence Detachment (Strategic), 200 Wintergreen Avenue, New Haven, CT 06515, 1993. (First made available [in the First Edition] at the Open Source Solutions Conference in 1993.)

4.   Ibid, 10.

5.   Ibid, 10.

6.   "Computer Security Is Not Protection, It's Delay," editorial, *Computerworld,* 3 March 97.

For More Information

I.   Other resources Rypka uses to keep informed (most of the resources mentioned below are available through the World Wide Web):

* Where Rypka finds information to improve his own technology capabilities and those of his clients in his specialized areas of knowledge are a combination of things, what he calls "sequential" information, "from the phenomena to the product," i.e., from trade associations to people/experts to equipment. He cites *Newsnet* (800-952-0122) for its specialized electronic newsletter database, which includes *Video Technology News, Mobile Phone News,* and all of the newsletters under the *Newsnet's* telecommunications category.

* He uses e-mail daily for sending and receiving messages and reports. "Gophers seem to be quite useful for searching expeditions, news groups, advice, or just about anything," says Rypka. "Gophers and FTPs should not be overlooked."

* He uses the Association of Independent Information Professionals Forum (members only) for discussions with information specialists who provide electronic and manual research support, and the *Burwell World Directory of Information Brokers,* which lists hundreds of researchers with specialized subject expertise. He also uses the SafetyNet Forum on CompuServe (GO SAFETYNET) for an electronic bulletin board in the area of law enforcement and safety.

* He also subscribes, in print or electronically, to several law enforcement publications:

Law Enforcement Technology (PTN Publishing, Melville, NY). Reports on a broad range of law enforcement technologies and related issues.

Computer Telephony (Computer Telephony Publishing, Nashville, TN). A magazine concentrating on computer-telephony integration technologies, applications, and issues.

State & Local Government Computer News (Cahners Publishing, Newton, MA). Reports on technological applications for state and local government problems, including software, hardware, imaging, GIS, data basing, and other issues.

- Law Enforcement associations are also an important source:
  - International Association of Chiefs of Police (IACP)
  - International Association of Law Enforcement Intelligence Analysts (IALEIA)
- Software for organizing and bookmarking Internet and World Wide Web resources:
  - Cybersearch, Frontier Technologies, http://www.frontiertech.com

II. Rypka cites another article on computer security which describes the looming crisis of digital nightmares: "Computer Information Insecurity, Issues and Answers Underscore Current and Future Dangers," *Contingency Planning & Management*, March 1997, Vol. 11, No. 3, pp 17-21. The article provides the mounting evidence:

The 1996 CSI/FBI Computer Crime and Security Survey revealed that 42 percent of more than 400 respondents (mostly from Fortune 500 corporations, financial institutions, and government agencies) had suffered incidents of unauthorized computer usage within the last 12 months. The survey also showed that more than 50 percent considered U.S.-owned corporate competitors a likely source of attack. Only 17 percent reported attacks to law enforcement agencies, citing fear of negative publicity as the primary deterrent.

And in the 1996 *Information Week*/Ernst & Young LLP Information Security Survey, it was disclosed that many of its 1,300 respondents had experienced financial losses from diverse security problems. For example more than 40 percent had experienced losses due to malicious acts by employees, more than 20 percent attributed to malicious acts by outsiders, more than 70 percent from inadvertent errors, and almost 30 percent had experienced losses due to natural disasters.

III. To contact Allan Rypka at his homepage, go to: http://www. radix.net/.

Chapter 13   A Provider of Library and Knowledge Management Services

Guy St. Clair

> The discipline of knowledge management is in its infancy. There will be an initial rush to embrace and adopt a knowledge management discipline without fully understanding its implementation require- ments or its underlying implications for the organizational culture. Simplistic efforts will be doomed to fail.
>
> J. Fenn, E. Stear, Gartner Group's *IRCM Research Note*, 1996

After graduate school at the University of Illinois, Guy St. Clair began a career in librarianship, working for public and academic libraries in Richmond, Virginia. He then moved to New York, where his first job was as librarian at the Union League Club, a private social club. "It had a handsome library," says St. Clair, "with a rare book collection and popular reading materials, as well as a famous collection of American art"—all of which were his responsibility to organize and maintain for the club's members.

After ten years at the Union League Club, St. Clair was recruited to become director of the University Club library, the largest private club library in the world, established in 1865, located on 54th Street in New York.

St. Clair's position at the University Club was unique, and he speaks of it warmly:

> The club's founders had realized the importance of a place for social intercourse, but they wanted to provide intellectual stimulation as well, so when they founded the club in 1865, the charter stated that the club be incorporated for "the purpose of the promotion of literature and art, by establishing and maintaining a library, reading room, and gallery of art." In addition to a bountiful collection of general reading materials, the library now includes a specialized collection of biography, the U.S. Civil War, antebellum Southern history, World War I and World War II, British and American literature, and a well-known and impressive rare book collection that continues to grow.

Mr. One-Person Library

In 1972 while still employed at the Union League Club, St. Clair was invited to speak in a round table discussion of 10 or 12 people about his experiences managing a one-person library. "By the time we opened the doors, there were people lined up down the stairs, through the lobby, outside and around the block," he said.

St. Clair saw this as an opportunity, and he began studying the subject of one-person librarianship as a distinct discipline within librarianship which no one had studied before. By 1984, he had started a company, OPL Resources, Ltd. (which stands for "one-person library"), and he and an associate, Andrew Berner, began writing and publishing a newsletter, *The One-Person Library: A Newsletter for Librarians and Management.*[1] In 1986, the book which he and Joan Williamson coauthored, *Managing the One-Person Library,*[2] was published and became an instant success.

The work that OPL Resources, Ltd. became involved in provided a welcome new focus for librarians, for although most librarians in training were prepared for careers as professional librarians, the educational emphasis had been on working in large public and academic libraries and similar multi-staff organizations. St. Clair's research demonstrated that as many as one-third to one-half of all people who work as librarians practice their profession totally alone, or with minimal support staff but with no other professional librarians in their immediate work environment. St. Clair took on the challenge of ensuring that these practitioners acquired and used the same management expertise that other librarians were required to use in their work, and as a result of his efforts in this area, St. Clair was awarded the Professional Award of the Special Libraries Association (SLA) in 1989, an award given only 30 times during the association's 90-year history.

Special Librarians: Strategic Players in Corporate and Academic Libraries Worldwide

Throughout his career, Guy St. Clair has always been an active participant in the workings of the "special libraries" community and was elected president of Special Libraries Association for the 1991-1992 term of office. The SLA is a 15,000-member organization of librarians and information professionals who specialize in over 30 separate subject fields of knowledge collection and organization representing business, science, technology, and the humanities. Most information-driven companies and many academic institutions with specialized and diverse research requirements worldwide employ special librarians. Some of the companies are AT&T, Apple Computer, Inc., Microsoft, Inc., Intel Corp., 3M Company, CIGNA Corporation, IBM Corporation, Ernst & Young, First Boston Corporation, Arthur Anderson LLP, Fidelity Management & Research Company, Solomon Brothers, Forbes, Inc., Procter & Gamble, General Motors Corporation, Hewlett Packard Company, General Mills, Inc., and the Los Angeles Times. Examples of universities with major research libraries that employ librarians with highly specialized skills include Johns Hopkins University, Massachusetts Institute of Technology (MIT), Harvard, Stanford, Yale, and most state universities.

During his presidency, the recruitment of highly qualified practitioners into special librarianship became St. Clair's rallying cry, for he was determined to change the common perception of librarians as "little old ladies in tennis shoes" to that of critical information providers or, as he likes to call them, "information counselors." In fact, at one of the SLA's annual business meetings, St. Clair was even so bold as to suggest to a dumbfounded constituency that the word "librarian" was inadequate to describe the work of the modern knowledge worker. "As long as we continue to call ourselves 'librarians,'" he said, "we will not be taken seriously by those whose influence and support we need."

St. Clair's early work, as well as that of many others, helped lay the groundwork for future definitions of the specialized information professional. In October 1996, the Special Libraries Association released *Competencies for Special Librarians of the 21st Century.*[3] This eight-page summary document spells out what the association identifies as the knowledge competencies and skills (both personal and professional) required in the areas of information resources, information access, technology, management, and research and the ability to use these areas of knowledge as a basis for providing library and information services. The entire report on competencies can be found on the Special Libraries Association Web site at http://www.sla.org. Note that the competencies are listed on pages 96-97 of *InfoThink.*

The Librarian as Entrepreneur

In his final speech as president of the Special Libraries Association, St. Clair challenged his constituency to become entrepreneurs who use business methods to survive in a rapidly changing environment, pointing out that special librarians are poised for leadership in the profession and in their organizations because of their working knowledge of both the information process and the information content. "By integrating information service into the organization, special librarians and other information services professionals can empower themselves to become strategic members in organizational teams," he summarized.

The Information Services Umbrella: One-Stop Shopping

St. Clair's empowerment theme became the subject of another book, *Power and Influence: Enhancing Information Services Within the Organization,*[4] published in 1994 as second in a series of books on information services management. In this book, St. Clair became a champion of a new concept in librarianship called the "information services umbrella." He explains:

> It is very important that librarianship be pulled away from its previous connections with education and social work and moved over into the areas of our society that are concerned with the delivery of information. What our information customers want is one-stop shopping. They want to go to one place, to a single information kiosk, ask their question and get the response they need. They don't care who gets the question, and they don't care where the answer comes from, whether it is in records management or the special library, whether it's pulled up from a file folder or an online database, or whatever. And they only want to ask the question one time. They just want the answer. That's the way information will be delivered in the future, and to protect themselves, I think librarians need to recognize this and accept that they are not a unique, stand-alone profession. We are all part of information services, and the sooner we recognize that and accept it, the sooner we'll be able to plan for our professional future.

Guy St. Clair's *InfoManage*

St. Clair's travels while president of the association opened many doors of opportunity. While the one-person libraries were still important, he saw an increasing need for consulting services to larger libraries and information agencies, such as records management and Management Information Systems (MIS) units.

In 1992, St. Clair established SMR International (St. Clair Management Resources International). The company provides management consulting, publishing, and training. Under the publishing unit, St. Clair's monthly publication, *InfoManage: The International Management Newsletter for the Information Services Executive,*[5] is worthy of particular comment because of its high information content. A main feature in the newsletter is "The Information Interview," which provides profiles and interviews with successful information executives, the leaders in the field. It is valuable because it documents the changes that companies and organizations are experiencing in the modern information delivery environment. The newsletter also identifies and explores emerging trends in information services and includes such subjects as knowledge management, the development of organizationwide information policy, the critical role of the information audit, and "partnering" among the various internal information delivery functions.

The Information Audit

The information audit is an important piece of the service that St. Clair's consultancy unit provides. The term "information audit" is not new, but it has historically referred to data being moved around within information systems. To St. Clair, the audit is more than just a "data needs assessment." It is connected to the strategic management of the company, he says, "and involves responsibility, accountability, and reliability on the part of the information service providers (in this case, the librarians) because management has to know why they have this operation (the library or information center, and now the Intranet) that is overhead, why it is costing all this money, and what they are getting for it."

Discovering the Flaws in the Delivery of Information

By the time St. Clair and his group are called in to conduct an audit, the organization is usually in trouble, i.e., nobody is getting the information they need to make decisions. Sometimes the problem is in the library, or it can be an organizationwide one. Many times, it is a management problem, because the organization's management has not been thinking about the delivery of information as the critical function that it is and usually doesn't realize there is an information problem until a malfunction in the information services operation brings it to their attention. Typically, it is someone at the senior management level who seeks out St. Clair and his "strategic partners" (i.e., information specialists), as he calls them, to work with the organization in solving an information management problem.

In order to develop an integrated information picture, St. Clair and his team will begin to ask questions such as: "Do you know what you are using information for? Do you have an information policy within your company? Do you know that you have a library in your company? Why aren't you using your library?" Or it could start in the library asking the librarian: "Why aren't they using your library?" Is the problem with the librarian or the client who needs the information?

Digging Deeper

After these initial questions are answered, St. Clair's team determines what it is that will meet the needs of the company and the librarians (or records managers or archivists or other information services unit staff being examined) within the company and how they can work together to deliver productive, usable information within the organization.

He begins by sending a survey to users, management, and other organizational or community personnel that asks about the use or difficulty of use for both internal and external information.

During the period of time the survey is being completed, interviews are conducted with selected members of the organization or community, either face to face with one person at a time or with focus groups. This kind of questioning is very valuable, St. Clair explains: "The goal of the interviews is to establish patterns of information-seeking behavior and service to clients within the organization. The whole point of it is that we want to 'open the floodgates.'"

When surveys are returned and the interviews completed, the results are tabulated and interpreted in light of organizational and community goals. Data are then analyzed, concepts are defined, recommendations are made. St. Clair describes his solutions:

> The final recommendations section might mention such things as: hire a chief information officer, start a policy group, develop a marketing plan, or focus on customer satisfaction. Most of the recommendations relate to information transfer and information flow, and they incorporate the information audit as part of the strategic plan of the organization, which relates to profit down the road, even though it is difficult to justify or measure at the time.

Documenting the Information

Needs of the Organization

St. Clair says that occasionally librarians conducting an information audit will be upset because they suddenly discover new users and/or requests for new or different types of information, and they become fearful of being overwhelmed with requests. But he emphasizes that one of the most important aspects of the audit is that it documents the needs for information and services and many times gives the librarian an opportunity to prove to upper management that the organization hasn't been taking advantage of tools, resources, and services it can use to get its job done. It is also an opportunity for the organization to become more aware of the information and services that it hasn't been using to get its job done.

The Critical Importance
of an Information Policy

Far better than most literature in the information services milieu, Elizabeth Orna's book *Practical Information Policies, How to Manage Information Flow in Organizations*[6] has guided St. Clair through issues of information management and how to achieve it. Her book explains how to integrate information policy into the key activities and objectives of an organization. It also explains how to set about developing a policy based on an information audit, and then it describes how to introduce, implement, and monitor the policy. Orna's summary is that the information audit looks at the information the organization holds, how the organization uses information, who manages information resources, and how these all relate to the management of the organization or the community as a whole. She then presents real case studies of information policies in major organizations such as Coopers & Lybrand, Glaxo, the British Library, and *USA Today*, and includes a generic case study for small firms.

St. Clair sees the information audit as a means not only to measure use of information, but to establish information policy within the organization and to help educate the companies about the contribution the information professional can make to the organization.

My goal is that every organization with an information unit of any kind, whether it's a records management team or library or strategic planning unit, have an information policy, just as they have a human resources policy or a financial investment policy. I think you cannot deliver information ad hoc. The traditional method, where you come in and ask me a question and I try to give you an answer, is short-lived. An effective information policy would give better performance and control throughout the corporation or organization.

Service Issues, Not Storage Issues

St. Clair believes that the effectiveness of information services needs to be measured more accurately. He is not referring to the economic value of information and services that many have tried to measure in terms of productivity and value —numbers. "The old 'warehouse' measures of how many books are on the shelf or how many database searches were conducted, is not enough for managers and power brokers within the organization," says St. Clair.

Rather, they want to know how their company or unit succeeded in their business or with this contract as a result of the library or information services unit and the information it provided. Or, in another typical situation, they want to know how much time was saved by utilizing the services of the library or information unit.

But he also observes that effectiveness measures are at present simply anecdotal and that is not enough:

It is not difficult to understand why it must of necessity be anecdotal. Since each information customer comes in with his or her own unique query, and since the analysis of that query in the information interview, together with the decision about strategies for procuring the information, always involves individualized and unique steps in the information delivery process, it is practicably impossible to establish a standardized measurement that will determine whether a service, product, or consultation has been effective or not. Some work in this area is being done in the health services information field, but quantitative, reliable effectiveness measures are still only in the very earliest stages of development.[7]

The progression of "informational events" over the past 30 years has led St. Clair toward higher levels of endeavor. He has had the opportunity to see the world's greatest libraries, to visit the inner sanctums of great book collections, and to see firsthand the challenges libraries and librarians are experiencing in the transition from providing print to providing electronic information in both large and small organizations. Establishing communication and links are most important to St. Clair, and his warmth combined with his "mentoring attitude" and a genuine and solid dedication to his profession have created a demand for his ideas and presence by corporate and academic librarians worldwide.

The Trend Toward
Knowledge Management

The next step for St. Clair has been to move into knowledge management. In a chapter about special libraries in *Library and Information Work Worldwide, 1997/98*,[8] he discusses the trend toward knowledge management and the integration of information into the organization. He cites a definition of knowledge management by Lois Remeikis, director of knowledge and information for Booz-Allen & Hamilton, who is considered a leader in the field of knowledge management:

> Simply put, knowledge management is the creation, capture, exchange, use, and communication of a company's "intellectual capital"—an organization's best thinking about its products, services, processes, market, and competitors. Closely related to a company's other information activities, knowledge management involves gathering internal information, such as financial and marketing data, and combining it with related external data, such as competitive intelligence. It goes beyond simple records management in that the information captured may include ongoing discussions, corporate stories, and other facts not typically documented.[9]

It is in the knowledge management arena that you will find Guy St. Clair in the future. In *InfoManage,* he says:

> What happens with knowledge management...is that it moves information services into a third realm, in which the organizational or corporate goal is not just the delivery of information, but the literal, seamless integration of internal and external information that links

What happens with knowledge management...is that it moves information services into a third realm, in which the organizational or corporate goal is not just the delivery of information, but the literal, seamless integration of internal and external information that links directly to the achievement of organizational success. A powerful paradigm, indeed.[10]

Notes

1. Guy St. Clair, *The One-Person Library: A Newsletter for Librarians and Management* (New York: OPL Resources, 1984).
2. Guy St. Clair (with Joan Williamson), *Managing the One-Person Library* (London and New York: Bowker-Saur, 1986).
3. *Competencies for Special Librarians of the 21st Century: Executive Summary* (Washington, DC: Special Libraries Association, October 1996).
4. Guy St. Clair, *Power and Influence: Enhancing Information Services Within the Organization* (London and New York: Bowker-Saur, 1994).
5. Guy St. Clair, *InfoManage: The International Management Newsletter for the Information Services Executive* (New York: SMR International, 1992).
6. Elizabeth Orna, *Practical Information Policies, How to Manage Information Flow in Organizations* (London: Gower Publishing, 1990).
7. Guy St. Clair, *Total Quality Management in Information Services* (London and New York: Bowker-Saur, 1995), 139-140.
8. Guy St. Clair, *Library and Information Work Worldwide, 1997/1998* (London and New York: Bowker Saur, 1998), in press.
9. Lois A. Remeikis, "Knowledge Management—Roles for Information Professionals," *Business and Finance Bulletin*, no. 101 (Washington, DC: Special Libraries Association), Winter 1996: 41-43.
10. *InfoManage: The International Management Newsletter for the Information Services Executive*, 3, 4 (New York: SMR International), September 1996: 4.

For More Information

I.   For further information:

- To view Guy St. Clair's homepage, go to   http://www.mindspring.com/~smrintl/smr.html
- For more information on the Special Libraries Association, go to http://www.sla.org

- *The One-Person Library: A Newsletter for Librarians and Management*, 11, no. 9 (January 1995).
- Guy St. Clair, "The Needs Analysis, User Survey, and the Information Audit," *Customer Service in the Information Environment* (London: Bowker-Saur, 1993).

Part 3   Information Educators and Pioneers

Profiles

In many respects, the information professionals—as intermediaries or providers of information—are the educators, the mentors, who provide guidance and direction through the information maze. In addition, there are educators and pioneers in the information sciences, in library schools, and in professional and trade associations who help students, faculties, and businesses adapt to new Information Age requirements in the workplace.

Steven Bell, Assistant Director, The Lippincott Library of the Wharton School, The University of Pennsylvania, Philadelphia, Pennsylvania
   Director of a business school library, Steven Bell provides a first-hand view of how business librarians at the Wharton School's Lippincott Library are accomplishing their mission to ensure that every student who graduates with an MBA or a business degree from Wharton knows what business information resources are out there and what basic skills are needed to retrieve these resources.

Patricia Senn Breivik, Dean, Library System, Wayne State University, Detroit, Michigan
   Patricia Senn Breivik, dean, educator, librarian, author, and early advocate of "information literacy," explains the concept of resource-based learning and how universities, schools, and businesses are beginning to recognize its value.

Paul G. Zurkowski, President, Ventures in Information, Chevy Chase, Maryland

Paul Zurkowski, a pioneer in the information industry, discusses the early events in the 1960s that would impact a new universe of information users and would engender new technologies for the organization and delivery of information. As founding president of the Information Industry Association, Zurkowski provides insight into his early efforts to help define the new information industry.

Paul Wasserman, Professor Emeritus of Librarianship, College of Library and Information Services, College Park, Maryland

Professor emeritus of librarianship, founder and former dean of a library school, professor, world-renowned researcher, and author on the subject of books, libraries, and institutions that house the written word, Paul Wasserman says that "connections"—not "collections"—will become a unique challenge for providers of business and information services in the future.

Chapter 14   A Director of a Modern Business School Library

Steven J. Bell

Few executives yet know how to ask: "What information do I need to do my job? When do I need it? In what form? From whom should I be getting it?"

> Peter Drucker, "Be Data Literate—Know What to Know,"
> *Wall Street Journal*, December 1, 1992

In today's world of business, it is a known fact that one cannot go very far without an MBA (Master's of Business Administration). For Web sites of one of the business schools that consistently ranks at the top of *Business Week's* prestigious "Best B-Schools," go to the Wharton School of the University of Pennsylvania at http://www.wharton.upenn.cdu, where in 1996, applicants to Wharton's undergraduate, MBA, and Executive MBA Programs all soared to new records; where only 15 percent of graduate school applicants were admitted; and where 99 percent of the graduating class had received job offers by graduation.

Once on the popular Wharton School Web site, then click on *Resources and Publications*, which will link you to the Lippincott Library where you will see links to such virtual resources and services as library catalogs listing books located throughout the library, multidisciplinary databases, reference tools, end-user services, and business Web sites worldwide.

Actual Libraries, Books, and People

How do such excellent business information resources and tools get from the library world to Wharton's Lippincott Library Web page? Who combines the local content? Who provides links to the best business Web resources available? Who tests and evaluates the sites before linking?

The page is a team effort guided by the library's Web overseer, the business reference librarians, and Steven Bell, the assistant director, whose job it is to make sure that both the actual library and the virtual library run smoothly.

Bell wears many hats. He supervises the day-to-day operations of public services, student hiring and training, and the reference and support staff for public services; he plays a part in print collection development by reviewing the many new print resources that are available; and he is also part of the team that reviews and monitors the electronic resources.

Bell started at Lippincott as a business reference librarian over ten years ago, and he has become a subject specialist in accounting, finance, health care, and merger and acquisition research. He also teaches "bibliographic instruction," now called "end-user instruction," an area the Lippincott Library pioneered in the 1980s by being one of the first university business libraries to offer end-user (students and faculty) services with access to commercial electronic online databases previously available only to professional searchers.

Wharton Demographics

Wharton's Lippincott Library and the staff who work with Steven Bell serve a large and diverse constituency, that is, the whole university of 17,000 students and faculty and the public as well. However, the main focus is on making the library's valuable resources available to a Wharton business university that include undergraduate, MBA, doctoral, and executive education students who come to Wharton to earn MBA degrees from more than 60 different countries and from such diverse backgrounds as the Israeli Air Force, Czech television, and the Ministry of Finance in

Japan. There are currently 64,000 Wharton alumni in more than 100 countries as of December 1996.

The MBA curriculum at Wharton emphasizes both fundamental business skills and multidisciplinary perspectives. There are 11 academic departments, ranging from traditional business fields such as marketing management and finance to contemporary areas such as legal studies, public policy, and health care systems. Twenty research centers focus on such issues as entrepreneurship, global competition, manufacturing, and risk management.

The Lippincott Mission: Business Information 101

Steven Bell explains that the Lippincott Library staff's aim is to ensure that all business school graduates are equipped to make good decisions in the world of business. Their goals are:

- To introduce students to the whole spectrum of information resources that will enable them to make good decisions
- To enable students to find up-to-date, timely, accurate information in all formats, including print, CD-ROM, the World Wide Web, and online databases
- To teach information content and the characteristics of the many different resources

"For example," he says, "when do you want to go to LEXIS-NEXIS; when do you want to use Dow Jones Text or Menus? When do you want to use ABI/Inform? When would you use a CD-ROM? or the World Wide Web? When are other, print or offsite (e.g., associations), the most appropriate? Nowadays, finding the best information is about making wise choices from a wide array of options—the winners know where it is and how to get it fast. The losers plod aimlessly and perform futile searches. Put simply, we try to develop winners at the information game."

Challenges to the Mission

Bell explains some of the challenges that Lippincott's business librarians face in training students to be users of business information in the fast-paced environment of Wharton:

> The students are under a lot of pressure. They are taking four or five courses. They are trying to get jobs. They are trying to maintain a social life or they have families. They are going to presentations. And we are competing for their attention.
>
> One of the things I want to say right up front is that I don't want to give the impression that we are turning students into great information resource people. We know that we're not going to get much time with them. The many different kinds of training we offer are mostly limited to one hour. If you do more than one hour, nobody's going to come or they're going to get up and walk out. You know—when an hour's up—they've got someplace else to go. So we work hard to make sure we make the most of our limited instruction time with the students.
>
> If you look at the library literature, there is much concern about teaching critical thinking skills to end users. We don't have time for that, and we can't fool ourselves into thinking that we can teach students how to think critically about information retrieval or teach them how an index is created. We are just trying to get out the basic message about what is out there, and what some of the basic skills are you need to do a better job.
>
> We would love to get some library instruction built into the curriculum, but we see top professors getting proposed courses turned down—so it's very tough to get connected into the Wharton curriculum. We look for every opportunity to get into a class to give some course-related instruction. That is when any library training is most effective—when the students need our training to help them complete a very specific assignment.

Changing Users' Perceptions

There are other challenges for the Lippincott staff, Bell continues:

> One of the most obvious training issues we see is that many of our students have already worked in environments where they have probably had exposure to some electronic information resources like

Dow Jones, or LEXIS-NEXIS. Many of our students become what I call "LEXIS-NEXIS centric," and they think the whole information universe revolves around LEXIS-NEXIS. We realize one of our jobs is to combat that and educate them that there are many other resources that they can use and that LEXIS-NEXIS doesn't have everything, because none of the systems can provide all information—although LEXIS-NEXIS does have probably ten times the usable information that is on the World Wide Web...that's why you have to pay for it.

For students who are already familiar with just one system, we teach them how to use it properly, because many know only the most basic ways to do a search. And in most cases, they are searching very, very ineffectively. They don't know any of the precision commands. They don't know what segment searching is. They don't know how to limit by date. Often they don't understand Boolean logic or that there are powerful search capabilities to locate retrospective data. They do know about "ands" and "ors," but they don't have any conception of proximity searching, field searching, or even using truncation. In most cases, they don't understand how to get beyond the most basic electronic libraries and files. Once they are introduced to it, it is our job to teach them to use it effectively.

The "Information-Is-Free" Mentality

Another long-existing challenge for teaching business information usage, Bell explains, is the "information-is-free" mentality.

It is now more common for university libraries to provide expensive databases to students for free (subsidized by the library). We have been pioneers in offering it free or at low cost to students for quite a long time. But by giving it to them for free, students don't feel as though they're required to do good searching. Students think nothing of spending two hours going through thousands of documents, "Who cares, I'm not paying for it," is the mentality. There is certainly no incentive to do good searching when you are offered something for free. It's not like someone is doing a fee-based search and they are going to be penalized very, very heavily for poor searching. Of course, when students graduate and work in the real world, many times they learn quickly that the good, focused information isn't free. We see no solution except to get them into a class where we can explain the economics.

Orienting Students to Find and
Use Business Information

The staff at Lippincott conducts a number of outreach programs, mostly at the MBA level. At the beginning of each semester, there is an "information fair," where staff hand out various kinds of information, show people the Lippincott Web site, and tell them what they have access to. Bell explains that when students first arrive at Wharton, they are offered an initial instructional session introducing them to the business library and taking students through all the different resources that are available. "We don't expect them to learn how to use it at that point. We are just telling them it's out there, so they will know about it," he says.

> For the first six months, the kind of work that they do is very regimented. They are not doing very much research at that point and what they do need is given to them by their instructors. By the time they need to know the electronic resources, they have forgotten what we showed them! Fortunately, a good number of the students do remember that the Lippincott staff is available to help with research projects.

Scenarios for Problem-Solving with
Electronic Business Information

Bell provides examples of the kinds of information problems students bring to the library and how they are solved:

> On occasion, we may work on a one-on-one basis with a student. For example, I had a student who wanted to know what merger and acquisition deals were performed by certain investment banks, that is, for what deals did these investment banks serve as the advisor to the target and acquirers [sic] in the deal. So I worked with him on that system. The student had taken the DIALOG® Classroom Instruction Program (CIP) training class that enabled him to have access to Knight-Ridder Information's international data bank called Data Star, which has a merger and acquisition database. But of course, he didn't know how to use it with precision, and his search at first was much too broad. We had to create search parameters such as time period, value of the deal, and targets in certain industries. I sat

down with the student and helped him structure the search. The outcome was that he got the information he wanted in order to move ahead with his assignment.

Students often aren't aware that they can download the information to a disk and that they can upload it into a word processor, he explains. Staff have to deal a lot more than ever before with many kinds of post-processing questions.

> Frequently, four or five students will meet with me (or another library staff member) and present a problem where they have to develop a strategy for marketing a product. They don't have any idea where or how to get started. We lay out for them the different services that we have. We would first take them through our Web site which links them through our gateway to LEXIS-NEXIS, Dow Jones, and ABI Inform. We always show them this site first, because we know it's a centralized location students can use for many different products.

If necessary, Bell will write out search strategies for the databases and tell students what files to use. He says that it all depends on the students, because some of them know more. But if they are really starting at "ground zero," he may have to do much more detailed search planning and preparation for them initially. If they don't have any experience or background in searching, he will make sure that they attend the Lippincott basic training session before they start any projects. And if they need something beyond what is presented, he will tell them what is available on other databases that they can access.

> Two students were working on a research project and trying to find information on hand-held computers or Personal Digital Assistants (PDAs) in an industrial application. We went through the whole spectrum, including CD-ROMs like Knight-Ridder *Business and Industry* and DIALOG's® *Marketful*, to find market research reports. Of course, the students loved it. Who wouldn't? And you know often, they are just amazed at how much information they can retrieve. It's very rewarding when we can help them find the answers to their questions and at the same time open their eyes to how much information there is. They are oftentimes overwhelmed. They also realize it takes much knowledge to efficiently locate and retrieve

information, which gives them more respect for the whole process as they take the time to learn to use the systems.

Outcome: Becoming Enlightened and/or Independent Searchers

After graduation, Bell says, some of Wharton's MBAs will be doing the information searching themselves, but a majority of them will go to consulting firms, accounting firms, banks, and large organizations that have libraries and information centers staffed with librarians who can do the searches for them.

> There are the entrepreneurs who go and do their own thing. And many of those do come back to the Lippincott Library to find information on how they can get access to DIALOG® and LEXIS-NEXIS and all the other resources they have learned about in the library. I'm sure some do become subscribers, and I'm sure some never use these systems again. We do get numerous alumni who come back and want to get access to our resources or who call us for advice. Of course, we can't let them have access to our databases, because these are only for current students and faculty. But we can put them in touch with commercial online services or in some cases get them connected with information brokers.

Outcome: Grateful Students and Corporate Librarians

Bell says that students are "very grateful" when they actually do sit down and take the time to learn, because there is much pent-up frustration. "We show them strategies for good searches so that they can get useful information, and they're usually most appreciative of that."

"If you talk to some of the librarians who work in the corporate libraries, they'll tell you that we're making the MBAs information literate and that makes their job easier, because the MBAs know the resources and know how to communicate what they want to the librarians," Bell states. "I've also heard a few horror stories about students who expect to use DIALOG® for free. Our corporate colleagues have told us more than once to make sure the students know it's not free in the working world."

Using the World Wide Web as a Research Tool for Business

Bell talks about student use of the World Wide Web at Wharton.

The Web is our distribution channel for Lippincott's primary electronic library resources as well as for the many other information resources housed in other libraries on campus. We have carefully selected links and organized our Web site so it's easy for people to use, and we have provided Web access all over the library and throughout the campus. Students and faculty can also access it from their home or office. We encourage Wharton students to use the Web as a resource for business information.

But there are problems that need to be addressed, he warns. For example:

Students encounter difficulty finding information on the Web. A student was trying to find information on the Web about a company whose name was a phrase. She didn't know how to search a phrase, and she was getting all kinds of garbage. I took her to a search engine called Alta Vista (http://www.altavista.com), and I showed her how to go into the advanced searching capabilities of Alta Vista that show how to enter a phrase, and she found much better information after that. Sometimes students know of one search engine, but they don't explore the capabilities of several to determine which works best for a certain kind of search.

"There are other problems in using the Word Wide Web as an information source," says Bell.

Information content is so important. You will find many articles in the library literature with respect to accuracy and validity of information on the Internet. It certainly is a problem, but that's not going to stop our business students from wanting it and using it. So we have to go with the flow.

It's a two-edged sword, that is, you want to make things accessible to the students at their desktop, but when you do that, you lose the ability to have any control over it. It is unlike DIALOG's® databases, for example, through the Classroom Instruction Program, where we can control it. We can require that a student who wants to use it take a training class before they even get on it; we require that they write out a search strategy; we check the search strategy; we make certain they're prepared and they know what they're doing. That's the way that professional online searchers have always done it, but students just want to get on and start typing anything that comes to their mind. And you know, that's just not effective or productive.

Print Resources at Lippincott

Bell explains that the Lippincott Library contains more than 220,000 volumes, subscribes to more than 4,500 serial and periodical titles, and receives financial reports from hundreds of major U.S. and foreign corporations. Special collections at Lippincott include historical corporate annual reports that go back to the late 1800s, and there are other invaluable historical resources, such as complete sets of original *Moody's Manuals*.

Anything that is not accessible through our Web site is going to get less usage now. But we're definitely maintaining our print collection, although in cases of print-electronic duplication, we'll drop some titles. This is now a big dilemma for us. For example, we spend much of our time these days trying to make decisions about how to deploy all of our resources. Do we go to the Web site version of the database? Do we abandon the print and CD-ROM resources? And while we know that there are disadvantages to the Web version of a database, nevertheless, students are going to appreciate remote access via the Web.

More and more, students don't even think about using appropriate business resources in print. They will come in to do research and ask where they can find the information on the Web. I'll say, "There is a book right here that has the information you need." In most cases, they just aren't aware of the fact that there are so many excellent print resources in the Lippincott Library. Many don't know that we have an automated card catalog of the entire library collection. I will say, "Did you search Franklin?" and they reply, "What's Franklin"?

But then some students have very specialized needs, especially the Ph.D. students. They're more sophisticated. They realize that they still have to use many books for their research.

Having said all that, Bell asserts: "We still have a very strong commitment as the stewards of our print collection, and we continue to add loads of books."

Surveying the Wharton Community's Information Usage Patterns

"We try to gauge what people are using, how much they know about the library resources, what's most important to them and of course, what they want that we don't already have," says Bell.

Bell and the Lippincott staff have learned some things from the surveys:

There is no question that delivering our resources over the Web has vastly changed library usage patterns, because we are now giving students and faculty so much information from remote sites that they don't have to come to the library. In that regard, they are becoming more productive; however, the numbers show that library usage is down, so they aren't taking advantage of many good resources that are available in the library.

An important drawback is that students are probably using the information we are providing them on the Web poorly. If I see someone using the Web resources in the library, I can look over their shoulder and say, "You know, you really could do a much better job on this." I can't do that for a remote user. So, we don't know how effectively they're using our resources.

There is a shift in what we as librarians do and how we reach people. For example, we have a librarian who would have spent much time on the reference desk in the past, but is now spending more time working on our Web site, looking for sources, evaluating sources, making modifications. To be sure, our job is more than disseminating information about LEXIS-NEXIS and the other databases. It also includes our communication to the users about the library, our training program, our hours, and our search guides. Since students aren't coming to the library as frequently as we want them to, producing guides on our Web site that will help answer their questions has become critically important.

More students are contacting us by e-mail to ask questions about how to do a search on various databases. I now respond to each student and give all the commands needed to find the information.

"The Web and the Internet have changed everything. I am sure you would hear that from anybody who is working in this profession. I think it is great, because information is becoming easier for students to access and they are learning more," Bell believes.

Gauging the Information Needs of the Wharton Community

There is a strategic disadvantage at Lippincott Library, because it is not in the building where the faculty and students are teaching and taking their classes, Bell says. "We are about two blocks away from the Wharton School itself, and that little geographic distance creates quite a difference in our ability to communicate with our constituents. But access to us through our Web site is helping."

Over the years, the Lippincott staff has developed various methods to gauge the information needs of the Wharton community. For example, there is a library committee that consists of faculty and students that "tells us what they think we need to be doing that we're not already doing," says Bell. He continues:

In addition to the committee, each member of the Lippincott Library staff is a liaison to one of the departments at Wharton. For example, I'm the liaison for the accounting department, and the faculty know they can tell me what they need. I think the librarians on our staff have a good sense of the kind of research students and faculty are doing because they know the curriculum very well. I know the kind of research accounting is doing so that if I have the option to get some kind of historical accounting databases, I know that nobody is interested in that, because they don't do historical accounting research at Wharton. Their research is more related to finance and quantitative research, so I am always on the lookout for that kind of information.

On the other hand, we [can't] give students and faculty everything they want. We're trying to make wise decisions about how to deploy our resources.

Determining student and faculty information needs is also based on outreach. Working at the Lippincott reference desk helps us learn what users' information needs are, and keeping in touch with the faculty in order to know when an assignment is due is helpful.

Technology Issues and Constant Change

Bell explains that changes in technologies are providing ongoing challenges and creating new relationships:

> You have to keep in mind that right now we offer our databases over a gateway so that 17,000 people can access it within the University. Take LEXIS-NEXIS or Dow Jones News Retrieval. We don't use the Windows software currently available for that, so it's kind of clunky. There's no point-and-click type activity. So, for students who are using these services from home, they have to configure their Netscape browser so that it will work with a Telnet client, and many of them don't understand that. That is a very interesting change that has occurred in the kind of work we do. Even though there are people coming to the library and we may not answer as many reference questions, we answer a lot more hardware/software questions such as: "How do I configure my browser? How do I set my parameters?" So, we've all had to become more computer literate than we were in the past.
>
> Even though the Wharton School has a whole computing office to answer these kinds of questions, many of them come through the library. On the other side, Wharton Computing gets a lot of questions from students about how to search LEXIS-NEXIS, so now we've been working with each other much more closely to understand what each other is doing, and we try to refer the questions to each other when appropriate. That's a big change.

How Lippincott Librarians Are Keeping up with Changes

"One of the many things we have to know is who's offering what," Bell says. "For example, we can't get into Investext on Dow Jones or LEXIS-NEXIS, but we can get it on DIALOG® or Newsnet. Right now, the database environment is in a state of flux—even more so than in the past. The standard resources are still there, but now you can find them in many other places where you couldn't find them before."

> I think it helps that we have a staff of experienced professional librarians, because nobody can keep up with everything. One librarian is our Dow Jones expert, and another is our DIALOG® contact person. We are all reading the vendor newsletters, and we read *OnLine* and *Database* and notices about new offerings. I think we make a good effort in this area.

There are now, and will continue to be, many changes with regard to accessing major database systems and other information resources through the Internet and the World Wide Web. Steven Bell says that as these events develop, the staff at the Lippincott Library will be formulating their information strategies to decide what works best to accomplish their organizational mission, which is to ensure that every student and faculty member at Wharton know what resources are available to them in the library and through the Web site, and to teach them the basic skills they need to resolve their information needs.

Thoughts, Observations, and Conclusions

Steven Bell comments on the future of librarians and on winning the information game:

> As far as "information agents" finding information on a specific topic where you need to gather information from a whole range of different resources (print, electronic, CD, Web, and commercial), I don't see them being able to do that kind of thing all that well. I think

you are still going to need someone who is very knowledgeable about the world of information resources. We see that to a large extent.

But our role is changing. And I am sure you have heard this in other libraries, too. Maybe we are not answering as many reference questions. Maybe more people are using our resources from home and not from our library. But what we *really* see more frequently is that people are confused. They know that a vast amount of information is available from their desktop, and trying to sort it all out leads to confusion. That is driving us more into the role of advisors and consultants. We know what's out there. We advise our constituencies that for the kind of information they want, here's what they need to do and here's how they do it.

Are we concerned that we are not getting as much in-library traffic? Yes. Are we concerned that even in the library, we don't get as many questions? Yes. Are we concerned that our users are using the great array of resources we've organized for them with less than stunning efficiency? Yes. What are we doing? Well, we are going on the offensive. If they don't ask us for help, we've got to be more aggressive and ask them if we can be of help. We're doing that right now—no more staying behind the reference desk. Get out on the floor and make yourself visible.

It is also an early stage of a transitional period. We are constantly learning how our users' information needs are changing in an age of rapid, diverse, electronic information dissemination and retrieval. It will take time to adapt.

We feel that the savvy students will take advantage of what we tell them, because they know they are going to save time. The ones who aren't savvy and think they can do it themselves are going to spin their wheels a lot. Maybe they will eventually get what they want, but it really goes straight to the bottom line: how much time and how much money it costs to get the information they need.

For More Information

Business School Information on the World Wide Web:

- Lippincott Library Business Reference Desk at http://www.library. upenn.edu/resources/business/busref.html links to libraries of business schools
- Marr and Kirkwood *Official Guide Links to Business School* Web sites worldwide at http://www.ssrn.con/BSchool/index.html

- *U.S. News* at http://www.usnews.com/usnews/edu/home.htm for annual business school rankings
- MBA Forum at http://www.gmat.org/opps200.htm to speak directly with representatives of graduate management schools worldwide
- *Business Information Sources on the Internet*—University of Strathclyde, Glascow at http://www.dis.strath.ac.uk/business/
- *@Brint Research Initiative* at http://www.brint.com/
- *Nijenrode University—The Netherlands Business School Webserver* at http://www.nijenrode.nl/nbr/
- The MBA Page at http://www.cob.ohio-state.edu/dept/fin/mba.htm for job links, case materials, online resources, etc.

Chapter 15   An Educator and Advocate of Information Literacy

Patricia Senn Breivik

To respond effectively to an ever-changing environment, people need more than just a knowledge base, they also need techniques for exploring it, connecting it to other knowledge bases, and making practical use of it. In other words, the landscape upon which we used to stand has been transformed, and we are being forced to establish a new foundation called information literacy. Now knowledge—not minerals or agricultural products or manufactured goods— is this country's most precious commodity, and people who are information literate—who know how to acquire knowledge and use it—are America's most valuable resource.

> *The American Library Association*
> *Presidential Committee on Information Literacy,*
> *Final Report,* American Library Association, 1989

Patricia Senn Breivik, a Doctor of Library Science (DLS) from Columbia University, and currently dean of the University Library System at Wayne State University, casts a wide net. When she talks to businesses and economic development organizations about the implications of information literacy for a strong knowledge economy, she often cites Herbert E. Meyer, former vice chairman of the CIA's National Intelligence Council and advisor to presidents on national security. Meyer wrote in his book, *Real World Intelligence: Organized Information for*

Executives: "It is clear that many companies do not know how to find and use information effectively and that every day lack of timely and accurate information is costly to American businesses.[1]"

Breivik also cites Roger G. Noll from the department of economics at Stanford University, who wrote *The Economics of Information: A User's Guide*.[2] She explains Noll recognizes the economics of information as a relatively new, rapidly expanding, and extremely important area of research and he advocates that "better education in how to use information is an essential component of rational public policy toward the information sector."

Affecting Policy Change

Breivik's net is cast even wider as founding chairperson of the broad-based National Forum on Information Literacy, an umbrella group of national organizations whose members include the National Education Association, the American Association for Higher Education, the National Governors' Association, the National Association of State Boards of Education, and the U.S. Small Business Administration. "It is through the Forum of member organizations that information is regularly shared about the theory and more importantly the practice of information literacy," she explains.

The Need for a Vision

Breivik believes in information literacy because the learning of information skills that are integrated within the curriculum will enable students to access, evaluate, and use information to become self-sufficient and self-directed learners "from the cradle to the grave." She is undaunting in her efforts to see that leaders in business and academics in high places understand what such literacy can do to improve the educational system and the work force through its implementation. "It is well under way and showing up more and more in the literature," says Breivik, whose résumé reflects her own writing and also her involvement in policy planning boards, task forces, committees, associations, focus groups, and councils related to information literacy over the past 30 years.

The high-profile Breivik throws a lot of energy behind her words. Her view of the world comes mainly from her experiences in academic environments, which include organizing, developing, and managing academic libraries. She describes the outcome of her efforts as "a wonderful experience to feel you are making a difference," and she believes people are beginning to change the way they think about information, "especially since the Clinton/Gore Administration excited people's imagination about the Information Highway" with the introduction of the National Information Infrastructure Initiative.

Information Literacy in Academia: Knowledge 101

One of Patricia Breivik's monographs, *Information Literacy: Revolution in the Library*,[3] coauthored by E. Gordon Gee, then president of the University of Colorado (now president of Brown University), was written in 1989 while she was director of the library at the University of Colorado at Denver. The book advocated that academic institutions look at their libraries as key learning resources on campus that could play creative roles in reforming instructional methods and provide quality learning and research to its constituencies.

As 1995-1996 president of the Association of College and Research Libraries (ACRL), an 11,000 member association of academic and research librarians, Breivik helped provide leadership for the organization in achieving its goal of "development, promotion, and improvement of academic research libraries, resources, and services to facilitate learning, research, and the scholarly communications process." In 1996, in Breivik's "Message from the President," she observes that one particularly promising aspect of ACRL's ability to influence the higher education environment has been its increased networking with other higher organizations through the newly established council of liaisons that include:

- American Association of Community Colleges
- American Association of Higher Education
- American Council on Education
- Association of American Colleges and Universities
- Association of Education and Communications Technology

- Council of Independent Colleges
- National Association of State University and Land Grant Colleges
- National Forum on Information Literacy
- National University Continuing Education Association

Information Literacy in the Elementary Schools

In 1994, Patricia Breivik and J. A. Senn (an educational writer/ consultant, former classroom teacher, and Breivik's sister) wrote *Information Literacy, Educating Children for the 21st Century*,[4] a book aimed at educators and administrators at the elementary school level. It was dedicated "to the elementary school principals who, despite all odds, are responding creatively to the nationwide demand for schools to prepare young people for lifelong learning in today's Information Age...as well as to the school library media specialists and teachers who work with them." The book provides examples of how information literacy programs are being implemented through resource-based learning, in which teachers move away from single-text teaching toward exposing students to real-world information resources and technologies.

A New Model: Moving from Teaching to Learning

Breivik points out in her book that information literacy and resource-based learning are not new. She calls it a learning mode wherein the pupils learn from their own interactions with a range of learning resources rather than from class expository.

Breivik says that resource-based learning was tied to the concept of information literacy as the outcome of such learning when the American Library Association Presidential Committee on Information Literacy issued its definitive *Final Report*[5] in 1989:

> Ultimately, information literate people are those who have learned how to learn. They know how to learn because they know how knowledge is organized, how to find information, and how to

use information in such a way that others can learn from them. They are people prepared for lifelong learning, because they can always find the information needed for any task or decision at hand.

Developing the Aha! Experience

Breivik sees information literacy as a practical way to move beyond the roadblock for student learning. It is a move to enhance current teaching/learning methods by adding the richness and variety of real-world information resources to students' experiences. Its position is that schools must train students not only to gather information, but to evaluate it and to discern how to use it effectively to meet their needs.

What kind of resources? What kind of experiences? In 1994, the American Association of School Librarians (AASL) provided sample scenarios in *Information Literacy, A Position Paper on Information Problem Solving*.[6] The scenarios were intended "to exemplify cooperative instructional efforts between teachers and library media specialists to demonstrate problem-solving skills by enticing students into interest in the topic, by encouraging cooperation and motivating students to explore, compare, integrate and reflect on conceptual structures through real life experiences." Here are some of those scenarios presented by AASL:

Scenario: Elementary students who are setting up a fresh water aquarium in their classroom during a study of aquatic life plan their class time with the teacher before they consult and work with the library media specialist to locate and use print and nonprint sources. They collect the materials, plants, and animals based on their completed research. The teacher and library media specialist locate biological data through the Internet and students confer with the local experts via telephone interview and Internet e-mail.

Scenario: Three students in the elementary school library media center are working at a multimedia work station completing a report of interviews with elderly community residents. They are incorporating stories about their community during World War I, photos of some of the community residents, photos of the community from that period of time, and a table with community population figures.

Scenario: A district staff development workshop is planned by a team of curriculum personnel, principal, library media specialist, and teachers. The workshop emphasis is on critical thinking skills. Information searches are completed in ERIC [Education Resource Information Center] and other national databases to identify research in the field, people as speakers, and resources for student use. Plans are completed, packets of information collated for distribution, and the workshop sponsored.

Providing Pedagological Support, Not Just Library Tools

Breivik explains that the "switching station" for the information literacy process is the library (or media or resource center) because that's where the print and electronic media resources traditionally are collected and housed within a school building or organization. It is within the library/resource center that the process of learning starts, with the librarians/media specialists understanding the needs of the teachers and their curriculum, the teachers understanding the resources in the library and in the community, and the administration understanding and supporting the overall importance of the collaboration. "This collaborative model works best," says Breivik.

Roadblocks and Solutions for Success of Resource-Based Learning

Breivik's book, *Information Literacy: Educating Children for the 21st Century*,[7] points out the barriers that must be overcome in implementing the resource-based learning objectives: fixed library schedules, teacher/staff resistance, inadequate resources, and impatience. It then suggests ways to overcome these barriers:

Staff Development. "It is so essential that nothing else matters without it. Ideally, staffing would consist of a talented and dedicated library media specialist who has the vision, communicates well, works well with teachers, and has both technological knowledge and knowledge of the curriculum. In other words, the media specialist needs to be a master teacher. (Aides and/or volunteers would free the media specialist's time to work with teachers and students.) But even with an in-house information expert, staff development for teachers is crucial to their being able to work collaboratively and effectively with library media specialists."

Resources. Quite obviously, there is no solid program without a quality collection of resources to enhance the learning process. Breivik cites an evaluative checklist found in *Information Power: Guidelines for School Media Programs*[8] that includes the following questions:

Does the collection support and enhance specific courses and units of instruction taught in schools?

For any unit of instruction, does the collection contain:

- a variety of media?
- materials that are current?
- enough materials for the number of users?
- materials that span reading, viewing, listening, and comprehension levels?
- materials that span the opinion/cultural/political spectrum, if required?
- materials of interest to students?

Equipment.

Automation and resource-sharing. This includes statewide library resources.

Programs. These enable collaboration among community members, public libraries, and businesses as an important part of sharing resources, expertise, and funding.

Assessing and Documenting Information Literacy Success in Schools and Colleges

The assessment movement within education ties a student's progress to the general education program or core curriculum. Breivik says that the Information Literacy Forum Task Force includes assessment as one of its major objectives: "to include coverage of information literacy competencies in states' assessment exams."

Breivik points to the papers of Ralph Wolff, associate executive director of the Accrediting Commission for Senior Colleges and Universities for the Western Association of Schools and Colleges

(WASC), as providing a foundation for discussions about the direction needed for changes in accrediting standards for academic libraries, and as offering further indication of the potential value of libraries in the teaching/learning process at all education levels.

The Wolff papers describe how academic libraries historically have been measured by descriptive and resource-oriented evaluation, with little documentation of the impact of the library on the lives of students and faculty.

> While questions about quality and effectiveness are difficult to form and to answer, more effective methods of measurement and assessment might include such things as: analysis of the library's relationship to the mission of the institution and evidence of how effectively the library was accomplishing its role; analyses of usage data, especially in a disaggregated format by school, program or discipline to establish appropriate comparative benchmarks; data and analyses of faculty usage or surveys of faculty perceptions of the library; analysis of the faculty's relationship to the library and the role of the library in curriculum and program development; analysis of student perceptions of the library; analyses of the interlibrary loan system—typical users, time for delivery, cost issues, etc.; evaluations of bibliographic instruction efforts; the impact of new technology on the library, and the relationship of the library to the institution's computer center.[9]

Accessing the Economic Benefits of Information Literacy in the Workplace

Relatively few substantial studies had been undertaken beyond the educational setting to assess and document the value of information literacy (information resources and information skills), as a tool for productivity and learning in the workplace until the report, *Special Libraries, Increasing the Information Edge.*[10] In it, Jose-Marie Griffiths and Donald W. King define "the information edge" as "the relative gain that can be accomplished through effective use of information by individuals, their organizations, and their countries. This edge can be increased by acquiring accurate and meaningful information, in the right dose, when needed, and at a reasonable cost."[11] Griffiths and King's work includes a compilation of 23 studies of users and services of corporate and government libraries and information centers, and four national surveys of over

10,000 scientists, engineers, and other professionals who responded to the questionnaires, as well as in-depth interviews relating to the usefulness, value, and impact of information and libraries from a variety of perspectives. The results show that nearly all users of information sources or services can be viewed as enhancing the following organization goals:

- Increasing productivity
- Performing work better and with greater quality
- Performing work faster

The findings also reveal a positive correlation between reading and/or library use as indicators of productivity, achievement, "The Information Edge," and the potential for "lost benefits" when an information infrastructure or policy is not in place.

Another survey of note relating to information literacy thinking in the workplace and evaluating the economics of large corporate libraries and information centers was conducted by Laurence Prusak of Ernst and Young Center for Business Information and James Matarrazo, dean of the Graduate School of Library and Information Science, Simmons College, and appeared in a special report, *Information Management and Japanese Success*.[12] Eight managers in large Japanese firms described the Japanese approach to acquiring, managing, and disseminating the kinds of information they consider to be critical to business success. The key points were:

- Japanese firms place a tremendous value on information and do not feel the need to justify information management expenditures.
- The mission of the information function is already aligned with the strategic thrust of the organization.
- Information technology is seen as an enabler for information management, not the primary component.
- Management of the information function is rotated among all company managers.
- Japanese management reads.

Information Literacy for Small Business

No area has been more neglected than that of the small business in defining and providing insight into specific information needs and uses. "Small businesses make or break with information," Breivik affirms. It may be that such a large number of small businesses fail in the first year because they have failed to do the homework of putting together a business plan or conducting a preliminary marketing study, or they are too busy getting started to have the time, staff, or money to gather or monitor information about changes with competitors or their markets.

Information Literacy:
A New Component of State and
Local Economic Development

"Information literacy is absolutely essential for business and economic development," says Breivik. She cites a measurement established by SchoolMatch,[13] an Ohio-based company that maintains an extensive database on public and private elementary and secondary schools. The database is used to help families or corporations relocate, because one of the most important criteria for parents choosing a site is the quality of the schools in the area. SchoolMatch discovered that "of all expenditures that influence a school's effectiveness including those for families, teachers, guidance services, and others the levels of expenditures for library and media services have the highest correlation with student achievement."

New Books by Breivik

Two new books on information literacy by Patricia Breivik are in press. The first is an updated and expanded edition of her first version of *Information Literacy, Educating Children for the 21st Century*, which was published in 1994. The second edition will be published by National Education Association Professional Publishing in Washington, DC. It will provide strategies and new examples of how resource-based learning is being implemented across the country. It is dedicated to elementary school principals, teachers, PTA organizations, and librarians in the school library media centers.

Breivik's second book will be published jointly by the American Council on Education (Washington, DC) and Oryx Press (Phoenix, AZ). The book, *"Student Learning in the Information Age*, is part of a series in higher education. It provides an in-depth examination of real-world, resource-based learning as an important new paradigm for higher education. In this book, Breivik highlights examples of colleges and universities that are already using this approach successfully and offers a framework to help educators create their own programs. It is written for college and university presidents, deans, faculty, and all campus information providers who are concerned with preparing students for lifelong learning.

Notes

1. Herbert Meyer, *Real World Intelligence, Organized Information for Executives* (Friday Harbor, WA: Storm King Press, 1991), 24.

2. Roger G. Noll, "The Economics of Information: A User's Guide," from *The Knowledge Economy: The Nature of Information in the 21st Century* (Nashville, TN: Institute for Information Studies, 1993-1994), 52.

3. Patricia Senn Breivik and E. Gordon Gee, *Information Literacy, Revolution in the Library* (New York: American Council on Education/MacMillan, 1989).

4. Patricia Senn Breivik and J. A. Senn, *Information Literacy: Educating Children for the 21st Century* (New York: Scholastic, 1994).

5. "American Library Association Presidential Committee on Information Literacy," *Final Report* (Chicago: American Library Association, 1989).

6. American Association of School Librarians, *Information Literacy, A Position Paper on Information Problem Solving* adopted from the Wisconsin Educational Media Association (WEMA) (Chicago: AASL, 1994).

7. Patricia Senn Breivik and J. A. Senn, *Information Literacy: Educating Children for the 21st Century* (New York: Scholastic, 1994).

8. American Library Association, Chicago, and Association for Educational Communications and Technology, *Information Power: Guidelines for School Media Programs* (Washington, DC: 1988).

9. Ralph Wolff, "Rethinking Library Self Studies and Accreditation Visits," in *Challenge and Practice of Academic Accreditation: A Sourcebook for Library Administrators* (New York: Greenwood Press, 1994).

10. Jose-Marie Griffiths and Donald W. King, *Special Libraries, Increasing the Information Edge* (Washington, DC: Special Libraries Association, 1993).

11. Ibid, 8.

12. Laurence Prusak and James Matarrazo, *Information Management and Japanese Success* (Washington, DC: Special Libraries Association, 1992).

13. SchoolMatch, Blendonview Office Park, 5027 Pine Creek Drive, Columbus, Ohio, 43081 (http://www.schoolmatch.com).

For More Information

I. For more information on the subject of information literacy, go to the following sites:

- National Information Infrastructure (NII)—http://www.nii. nist.gov/
- American Association of School Librarians (AASL)—http:// www.ala.org/aasl
- Association of College and Research Libraries (ACRL)— http://www.ala.org/acrl
- Association of Research Libraries (ARL)—http://arl.cni.org
- Eric Clearinghouse publications on Information Literacy— http://www.ed.gov
- American Association for Higher Education—http://www. aahe.org/
- National Forum on Information Literacy—http://www.ala.org or e-mail: infolit@ala.org
- Educom—http://www.educom.edu
- National Education Association (NEA)—http://www.nea.org
- Association of Curriculum Developers (no URL address currently available)

II. Top Ten Information Literacy Sites on the World Wide Web by Dane Ward, November 14, 1996:

- Big Six Skills homepage
  (http://edweb.sdsu.edu/edfirst/bigsix/bigsix.html)
- Calico INFOLIT homepage
  (http://www.sun.ac.za/local/library/calico/infolit/)
- Information Literacy
  (http://www.uwsp.edu/acad/math/infolit2.html)
- Information Literacy and Resource-Based Learning
  (http://www.lib.fcu.edu.tw/~library/aeslink/i-literacy.html)
- Information Literacy Group
  (http://www.uclagary.ca/~jsday/its/ILG/ILG.html)
- Information Literacy Skills Program homepage
  (http://www.gu.edu/au/gwis/ins/infolit/home.htm)

- InfoZone
  (http://www.mbnet.mb.ca/~mstimson/)
- Internet Classrooms
  (http:www.rims.k12.ca.us/SCORE/classact.html)
- Ocotillo Reports
  (http://hakatai.mcli.dist.maricopa.edu/ocotilo/report.html)
- Winhall Elementary School Library
  (http://www.wcsu.k12.vt.us/~winhall/lib_1.htm)

III. Gates Library Foundation—the $400 million foundation established in 1997 by Bill Gates and his wife, Melinda, so that public libraries will be better able to provide all citizens the hardware, software, and training to access digital information. The foundation will become an enabler of both computer and information literacy. Go to http://www.glf.org/.

Chapter 16   A Pioneer in the Information Industry

Paul G. Zurkowski

The medium, or process, of our time—electronic technology—is reshaping and restructuring patterns of social interdependence and every aspect of our personal life. It is forcing us to reconsider and reevaluate practically every thought, every action, and every institution formerly taken for granted.

Marshall McLuhan, *The Medium Is the Message*, 1969

Paul George Zurkowski's biographical sketch in Marquis' Who's Who in America[1] lists him as an information company executive with an LL.B. from the University of Wisconsin; a publisher, investigator, and examiner for the Interstate Commerce Commission; a congressional legislative assistant; and an attorney in individual legal practice. It also mentions that in 1969 Zurkowski was executive director of the Information Industry Association, served as the Association's president from 1972 to 1989, and was named to the Information Industry Hall of Fame in 1988.

Who's Who doesn't mention that Paul Zurkowski had an instinct for information; that he got his best grades in law school in patent and copyright law; that in the 1960s he studied Marshall McLuhan's visionary works that coined the futuristic phrases "The Global Village" and "The Medium is the Message." Nor does it mention that he was on Congressman Bob Kastenmeier's staff in the late 1960s when Bob took over the chairmanship of the Subcommittee on Copyright Revision, "an issue that few knew about or understood, because it had to do with computers and the impact of the new technological uses of copyrighted works," he says. As president of the Information Industry Association, he would become knowledgeable on these issues and testify numerous times to CONTU, the Committee on the New Technological Uses of Copyrighted Works, which eventually led to revised legislation in areas of copyright that would impact a whole universe of users of information and would launch new industries.

Behind his biographical information is an important story about an Information Age pioneer who during the 1960s knew the avant garde of the publishing industry and emerging computer-based information content industry, to whom he refers as "an inspired bunch that penetrated mysteries." "Information people," he calls them, with "high information valences," people with enhanced capacities to link what they know in new and creative ways.[2] It may be important to know that he and William T. Knox, then vice president of McGraw Hill and later director of the National Technical Information Service in the Department of Commerce, met at the Cosmos Club in Washington in 1968 to lay out the parameters of an organization that could represent information businesses in a new industry, "to bring the various players together so that they could know each other and deal with each other." That organization came to be named the Information Industry Association and Zurkowski was key to its creation and development.

The Significance of Sputnik

Distanced by time from those early days in the information industry and now running a publishing company in the Washington suburbs, Paul Zurkowski recalls a signal event that sparked commitment, investment, and excitement about information. Sputnik was launched by the Soviets on October 4, 1957, and challenged the American scientific and defense communities to think more about who was in control of the information switch box.

"Rightly or wrongly," he says, "Sputnik alerted these communities to the superior information handling capabilities that the Soviets were thought to have."

He also explains that this new way of thinking about information prompted Hubert Humphrey, then a junior senator, to take legislative steps to create a national information handling capability to cope with the continually growing flood of scientific literature. Humphrey chose as the instrument of national policy the professional societies, the natural repositories of knowledge accumulated in their respective fields. His legislation created the Office of Science Information Services within the National Science Foundation (NSF) and authorized the new office to engage in providing information services. The funding supported the automation of the knowledge accumulated in publications such as *Chemical Abstracts*, *Biological Abstracts* (now *Biosis*), *Engineering Index*, *Psychological Abstracts*, and the American Institute of Physics, the American Mathematical Society, and such entities as the Geological Society.

The Politics of Information

In practice, Humphrey's legislation funded the development of information handling capabilities exclusively within the nonprofit sector, and private companies seeking to do the same thing objected to the spending of their tax dollars on strengthening their nonprofit competitors.

Thus, in addition to copyright issues over how to treat information content in new formats, and the simple need to figure out how to apply computers and other technologies to the creation, marketing, and distribution of information, there also was a need for a national voice to address the flood of new policy innovations such as the Office of Science Information Services. That voice came from the new Information Industry Association and helped to shape and chart the emerging industry.

The Information Map

Paul Zurkowski explains that one of his early accomplishments as president of the association was to set up the organization as a catalyst for stimulating discussion to help new members in the private sector understand issues and prepare for developments in the Information Age. "Integrating America's Infostructure," an article by Zurkowski published in the *Journal of the American Society for Information Science*,[3] helped define the emerging industry. In it, he described the "infostructure"—a play on the term "infrastructure"—as "the myriad elements necessary to support the sophisticated information handling capability that distinguishes the United States economy, enhances its productivity, and challenges our available human talent to be all that it can be."

The "Integrating America's Infostructure" article provided the visual representation of the infostructure in the form of an information map originally developed in the early 1980s by Harvard professor Anthony Oettinger to illustrate the relationship of various parts of the industry to computers. Zurkowski, however, adopted a distinctively different map—developed by Larry Day (then at the Denver-based Information Technology Group), who wanted to show information *sectors* and their relationships.

Zurkowski's version of Day's map (Figure 16.1) shows eight industry segments, each with their sectors (clockwise):

Figure 16.1 The Information Map

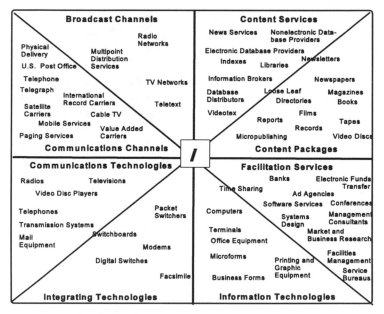

- Content Services
- Content Packages

- Facilitation Services
- Information Technologies
- Integrating Technologies
- Communications Technologies
- Communications Channels
- Broadcast Channels

Zurkowski observes that the map needs revision because there are many different players now. But at the time he wrote the article, he says, the map provided a way of looking at eight information industry segments "with the key force for integration being the information content that holds business in these eight sectors together and gives them their raison d'etre."

In *Critical Issues in the Information Age*,[4] which was based on a collection of seminars presented by the American Federation of Information Processing Societies series during 1985 and 1986 (with a foreword by Senator Albert Gore, Jr.), Zurkowski described the significance of the Content Services (services and packages):

> The most important point, though, is the message, the information content itself, that pulls us all together—not only all of us in the industry and all of those in society, but the people using information. Information content is the commodity we all relate to. It is as much responsible for generating income as the switch, a CRT, a compact disk, or a book, and since we are in business to sell and make profits, we should realize how valuable, how important, what we sell is.[5]

He further explains his thinking about the infostructure and the value of content:

> The integrating force for the infostructure is the need to move information content. The key to understanding the integration of all the diverse parts of the infostructure is the recognition that the objective of the Infostructure is to create, communicate, and deliver information useful to all the economic, social, and political activities of the country.[6]

Understanding Basic Information Principles

Zurkowski says that he feels privileged to have participated in the early stages of the Information Age, but he laments how much of its original focus and enthusiasm have been lost. He notes that the Information Industry Association will celebrate its 30th anniversary in 1998, and that, over those 30 years, the participants in the industry have learned the fundamentals of the information business. But "there are still indications that important 'principles of information' have not been communicated to society or business—that information content (not just technology) generates wealth; that failure to recognize this principle accounts in a significant way for economic problems; and that quality, value-added information content cannot always be free."

Documenting History: Back to the Future

There are many reasons that these principles and others have not been recognized or communicated to society. These are complex and both require and deserve a backward look to get "back to the future." Zurkowski says that he has always wanted to document the lessons that might be learned ("wishful thinking, perhaps"), from the personal histories of the information industry's founders and pioneers:

> There are people like Jim Adler, who created Congressional Information Services, the company which had people literally on roller skates running from congressional office to congressional office to get congressional documents to abstract and index, organize, and microfilm. And there is Curtis Benjamin of McGraw Hill, "the godfather of the Information Industry Association"; and Sam Wolpert, president of Predicasts; and Jim Kollegger, then president of Environmental Information Center, Inc. and founder [with Zurkowski] of the Associated Information Managers (AIM); and Dr. Eugene Garfield, of the Institute of Scientific Information (ISI), Roger Summit of Lockheed (now DIALOG® Information Services/ Knight-Ridder, Inc.), and Carlos Cuadra of SDC Search Services, all

key players in the launching of the electronic online industry, all with important stories to tell about the knowledge gained through their experiences.

Mankind's Better Moments
or Gresham's Law?

In the very early days of the Information Age, it was Paul Zurkowski's fate and good fortune, he claims, to interact with members of an industry dealing in information, those who were identifying, codifying, recording the ideas and artifacts of human existence, and making information available in machine-readable form through new technologies so that it could link to new knowledge—not just for edification, but for identifying and inventing tools "to deal with all life's complexities." He says that it was an exciting time working with those "who were very thoughtful about their information counterparts and what those information counterparts represented and how they relate to human beings."

Was that time in the Information Age one of those that historian Barbara Tuchman refers to as "Mankind's Greater Moments"?[7] Or has the Information Age evolved to now be a victim of Gresham's Law, in which "bad money" drives out good? Has life become more enriched or just more complicated?

Zurkowski thinks it ironic that just as the Internet scene is exploding, the information business, based on serving niche markets, is so fragmented and balkanized that there are neither interest nor funds in the budgets to sustain the education of the general public about the wealth-generating functions of this "invisible" industry—"literally the key to future human development."

"This situation is exacerbated," he says, "by the fact that hardware and telecommunications people, who spend huge sums of money on technological and the regulatory challenges, are not equally concerned about the content that flows through their computers and telecommunications equipment. Once you enter this hardware environment, you tend to lose sight of information content, of the library, and of intellectual property, of information itself."

The Essence of the Information Industry Business

Looking back as one of the pioneers in the information industry, Paul Zurkowski synthesizes some of the important issues and ideas that came from his experiences.

On what distinguishes the information industry from data processing, from information technology and from records management:

> Data processing applies information principles and practices to processing information owned and created for the owners' purposes and uses, usually in the normal course of events in a given enterprise.
>
> Information technology concentrates on managing information interactions between computers and communications largely for others.
>
> Records management initially directed its energies toward tracking information in particular media, paper records, microfilm, etc. Now it faces the challenge of storing, processing, and retrieving specific information in the new machine-readable storage form, but primarily for the benefit of the owner of information, not generally for the public at large.
>
> The information industry, on the other hand, is engaged in creating a machine-readable equivalent or counterpart, an information duplicate of every event, person, idea, artifact of human existence, most often on a for-profit basis to serve a specific constituency or market. Like ink-print publishers, the purpose is to profit from information transactions, to share the information with all comers and to facilitate the functioning of society through widespread access to and use of such information equivalents or counterparts. Competition is vital to the information business because no one entity can possibly imagine all the ways information needs to be packaged and presented to serve its many and different real and potential users.

On maintaining the integrity of information:

> In all of these cases, maintaining the integrity of the information involved is of paramount importance.

On utilizing information equivalents, counterparts, or duplicates:

> The congressional legislative process involves a huge printing effort by the Government Printing Office, but it was only 25 years ago that an information company, Congressional Information Service, recognized that no index existed for congressional documents and undertook the process of capturing the output of congressional agencies and making it widely available to the public through an ambitious cooperative effort with the library community. Suddenly, by creating all information equivalents or counterparts, the list of expert witnesses testifying before Congress and their testimony and responses to specific questions asked by members of Congress and their professional staff members became readily available across the country for everyone to access beyond the specific committees where they appeared.

> What distinguishes these information equivalents of the legislative process from the hearings reports and committee reports is that individual snippets of testimony or Q and A are now indexed and organized to be instantly accessible through electronic and digital means. A congressional candidate, creatively working with the information equivalents of the last session of Congress, can organize a well-articulated legislative program based on the identity and testimony of specific witnesses, as well as the committee report language spelling out a specific legislative objective. Congressional Information Services created a duplicate counterpart or equivalent of the entire legislative process. It is now time to create new ways of using this output in the daily lives, not just of congressmen and women, but of every member of society.

> Medical information equivalents offer perhaps an example that is closer to home. Because of the abundance of plain-language information services available in libraries and online, everyone can research and play out alternative treatment approaches taking into account side effects, expenses and anticipated recovery rates, the identities of specialists and their success rates with treatment procedures. The advantage to the individual patient is that the treatment approaches can be played out without the patient having to undergo surgery or a drug intervention until after the modeling of the treatment approach has been completed.

> Full use of these kinds of information capabilities awaits the development of methods to apply them to everyday applications, just as the full development of the computer's potential depended for most on the development of applications software. For most people, these information capabilities are like a genie in the bottle waiting to be let out.

On Marshall McLuhan's anti-environment:

> Society is constantly working to figure out all the inter-
> relationships between the myriad of people, artifacts, ideas, and
> activities which make up today's world. The race is on now to
> capitalize on the capability of dealing with the world's wealth of
> machine-readable information equivalents or counterparts.
>
> How will this be done? It will involve an equal set of
> relationships requiring resolution and adjustments to "real world"
> relationships. McLuhan suggested that in a period of rapid techno-
> logical change man needs an "anti-environment" within which he can
> play with the elements of his environment to determine who he is and
> what he is doing. Econometric modeling was once seen as a vehicle
> for managing the economy. With the products of information now
> available to be used in similar modeling of human choices, whether
> in war or social engineering, an exciting future vista is opening before
> us. This across-the-board capability offers the hope of being able to
> play out various scenarios using information equivalents that avoid
> the hazards to society of a disruption in the process.

On choices for the future:

> This capability will emerge as a way for every human being to
> exercise greater control over his or her choices, his or her life. It is not
> a simple matter, but it is within reach and will become easier as the
> process is demonstrated for us.

And finally, Zurkowski talks about what he calls "the grand experience":

> No one can ever imagine how much information there is. And
> because we are creating an information equivalent of all creation that
> denotes the immensity of relationships, we can't expect [adaptation
> to it] to be resolved in 30 years. Scientists are skilled in relating the
> characteristics of elements and compounds. Diplomats become
> instinctive about affairs of state and relationships between peoples
> and governments. Lawyers are trained and experienced in legal and
> social relationships of people in everyday, as well as the most com-
> plex, situations. Business people must master many production,
> distribution, and marketing relationships. Financial advisors operate
> in an environment epitomized by the trading volume on the New
> York Stock Exchange, which averages close to a half billion shares
> traded a day. Their entire work life is performed in most cases on a

fiduciary basis, in information equivalents or counterparts of stock ownership or other financial instruments.

These skilled workers and professionals are some of the first people in our society to be served by "wraparound" information services. These niche markets, in effect, have been the beneficiaries of the new development, because information companies have recognized the proportionality between decisions made in these fields and the value of the information needed to make the decision. Information has value in direct proportion to what is at stake in a decision—a key factor in generating wealth from information.

What determines who can take advantage of these capabilities?

Depending on education, training, and experience, each person has an information valence which controls what he or she can do, be, or become just as elements have a valence that controls which elements can combine to form what new compounds.

It goes beyond information literacy (knowing what information exists and where and how to find it) to a new level of creativity in developing wraparound applications for information resources in specific fields or applications. For many, it involves learning whole new ways to do their work.

The creation of the worldwide bases of information equivalents or counterparts adds a new dimension to life requiring everyone to recognize and deal with the consequences of this development or be left behind.

This work has only just begun and will always be, just like evolution, a work in progress.

To an industry which essentially teaches people about their information relationships, it is exciting to realize that as people learn something, they live differently.

Notes

1. Harriet L. Tiger et al., eds., *Who's Who in America 1997*, 51st ed., (New Providence, NJ: Marquis, Reed Elsevier, Inc., 1996), 2: 4735.

2. Daniel N. Lapedes, ed., *Dictionary of Scientific and Technical Terms* (New York: McGraw Hill, 1969). The "valence" in Zurkowski's "information valance" is adapted from the scientific term used in biochemistry—"The relative ability of a biological substance to react or combine; in chemistry—A positive number that characterizes the combining power of an element for other elements as measured by the number of bonds to other atoms which one atom of the given element forms upon chemical combination."

3.   Paul G. Zurkowski, "Integrating America's Infostructure," *Journal of the American Society for Information Science* 35 (May 1984): 170-178.

4.   Robert Lee Chartrand, *Critical Issues in the Information Age, Based on a Series of Seminars by the American Federation of Information Processing Societies, 1985/86.* (Metuchen, NJ and London: The Scarecrow Press, Inc., 1991).

5.   Ibid, 177.

6.   Paul G. Zurkowski, "Integrating America's Infostructure," *Journal of the American Society for Information Science* 35 (May 1984): 171.

7.   Barbara W. Tuchman. *Practicing History, Selected Essays* (New York: Alfred A. Knopf, 1981).

For More Information

For access to the Information Industry Association Homepage, go to: http://www.infoindustry.org.

For access to Web sites on Marshall McLuhan, go to: http://www.mcluhan.utoronto.ca and http://www.mcluhanmedia.com/mmclm001.html

Chapter 17   A Professor Emeritus of Librarianship

Paul Wasserman

If there is to be a new breed of librarianship, it will build on a perspective which sees in librarianship the capacity to satisfy the information requirements of human beings.

Paul Wasserman
*The New Librarianship, A Challenge for Change,*1972

One of his students referred to him as "a well-read, scholarly man, who also has an interest in business." He is known on campus as a "walking encyclopedia," and some even call him "The Godfather." He is a gentleman and a scholar with "a couple of Fulbrights," he says rather nonchalantly. His 14-page curriculum vitae mentions professor, administrator, librarian, chairman, lecturer, director, consultant, representative, advisor, instructor, and managing editor. His information theories are based on places where he has performed these functions, such as Mexico, the Philippines, Turkey, Central America, Chile, Ghana, Spain, Egypt, India, Nigeria, Germany, Sri Lanka, Thailand, and most recently Russia, Poland, and China.

Over 25 years ago when Dr. Paul Wasserman sat down to write *The New Librarianship, A Challenge for Change,*[1] his library science students spent much of their time wandering through the stacks and leafing through card catalogs. The Internet and CD-ROMs might as well have been the names for science-fiction civilizations.

Today the librarian's world is zipping full-speed into cyberspace on the information superhighway. It's the end of the line for librarians, right? Wrong.

According to Wasserman, professor emeritus at the College of Library and Information Services at the University of Maryland at College Park, and former dean of the college, such misconceptions about technology tend to create a skewed view of the role of the librarian. Wasserman is tackling these and other problems in his revision of *The New Librarianship,* in which he defines his vision of what librarianship will (and could) be in the 21st century.

"Being a librarian today takes a more proactive mind," says Wasserman, a soft-spoken man who speaks matter-of-factly about the survival of librarians in the information world. "A librarian has the potential to shape the intellectual waves of society, but too many students are put off by that responsibility. I like to encourage it."

The New New Librarianship

Much of the material for the prospective new edition of *The New Librarianship* comes from courses and seminars he has offered around the globe over the years. One seminar, "Inventing and Designing Information Products and Services," is taught to foster proactive techniques of information usage, Wasserman explains. "Normally the instructor imparts knowledge and the student builds some understanding of it. My course puts the shoe on the other foot. Here, the *student* has the responsibility to work toward fashioning a product. My job is to catalyze their ideas, react to what they're up to, help them shape a perspective, and identify outlets for their potential publication or product. Many in librarianship don't know what goes on in the development of the information products they use, even though they may work with them throughout their lives," he says. "It is something they need to know about." Some of the "products" conceived and developed include a handbook of 900 telephone numbers, a resource book for small business people looking to develop contracts with government agencies, and a reference work focusing on all aspects of telescopes.

A Life in the Library Sciences

If anyone is capable of redefining the concept of the library in the wake of the Information Age, it is Wasserman. He received two masters degrees from Columbia University, one in economics and one in library science, and a Ph.D. in library administration/public administration from the University of Michigan. He was a postdoctoral scholar in data processing and information retrieval at Case Western Reserve University and has worked and taught at institutions such as Cornell and Case Western Reserve. In 1965, he came to the University of Maryland to found its College of Library and Information Services and has been there since.

In addition to his forward-thinking new book, Wasserman has developed many of the innovative information products in the field. He has compiled and edited innovative statistical resource books, encyclopedias of legal information, and reference works on public affairs, senior citizens, and consultants.

The bulk of Wasserman's efforts has gone to creating usable resources for the business world, a world that has always been fascinating to him. His *Encyclopedia of Business Information Sources (EBIS)*[2] was a pioneering effort in the category of business information and is still considered a standard reference tool in libraries. "The book constitutes a jumping-off point for a fairly large number of subjects," he says. "It is designed for someone who doesn't know about the topic and wants to be informed about where to go." It contains references to periodicals, newsletters, statistics sources, trade associations and professional societies, research centers and institutes, online data bases, directories, and other sources, all relating to a specific topic.

"Many of my information products came into play when I was looking something up and couldn't find the appropriate information," claims Wasserman. "I knew that I could calculate a strategy for shaping such works myself."

The Internet and the Hula Hoop

The development that is foremost in most people's minds when talking about the Information Age today is computer technology. Gluttonous amounts of information are now available to anyone with access to a computer, a CD-ROM drive, and a modem—information that used to be the sole province of librarians.

"The Internet is significantly changing the world, and things are moving very quickly," says Wasserman. "More and more printed publications are being transferred to electronic versions, and that's changing how we deal with things. Technology has a kind of fascination like the hula hoop did in society long ago. These things are new and they're different and they have promise that will transfer to important applications to their businesses. It's stimulating interest in information that people weren't particularly interested in before."

Yet all the same, Wasserman believes that technology is only one aspect of library science, an aspect that has been given disproportionate coverage by the media. The result is a generation of people who mistakenly believe that jumping onto the Internet will solve all of their information needs.

"What we're getting in library education today is too high a premium on the development of technology," says Wasserman. "Everyone's fascinated with the process rather than the content. We don't have a fascination with what's under the hood of a car, we just drive. Technology is a vehicle, it's a device, it's a technique."

The bottom line, he believes, is that no matter how much information is out there for us to retrieve, technology can't solve all of our problems. "We have more and more information coming at us, but we can't absorb it any faster than we could a generation ago," he says. "This great proliferation of information doesn't necessarily make us more effective, because we can only read so much at a time. People are getting frustrated and saying, 'There's so much coming at me. I'll just turn everything off and fly by the seat of my pants.'"

Connections, Not Collections

Wasserman complains that a library culture that has so long been a fixture in American life has become resistant to change. Isolated from the law of supply and demand that is slowly pushing the traditional library out of business, the time has come to adapt. "The point of a library is not to make collections. The point is to be highly sensitive to the needs of the people who are using the library. Sometimes that means having very few books and using other access points to get at the information they're looking for."

"One of the best access points available that's often overlooked," he continues, "is people. It's always much more efficient to turn to a person instead of a book. That's as cheap and as current a source as you can get. We have innumerable knowers in government who are specialists and experts in all kinds of things, and they're public servants, they're there for us. If one wants to know about the current market price of jute, don't waste time trying to look it up. Call someone in the Commerce Department who's the world's authority on jute and ask."

Special Libraries: The Wave of the Future

With more and more information accessible to the average computer user, the idea of a library as simply a repository of knowledge is becoming obsolete, Wasserman believes. "The libraries that will survive the information revolution are special libraries, i.e., those that serve the specialized knowledge needs of their constituencies. The special librarians are those who are equipped to relate information resources across a wide range of specialties. They will possess the technology and knowledge skills that relate to the specific information needs and requirements of the corporation or institution. In a company or a government agency or an investment house, who wants a library"? Wasserman asks. "What you really want are intermediaries who link you up with the specific information you need to do your job right. Many librarians boast about how many volumes they have, but that just makes the information you need harder to find. In a special library context, if the librarian doesn't do this, and do it quickly and smartly, his/her days are numbered and so is the library itself. [Author's Note: There are librarians who can relate true stories of how their libraries were shut down and the collection thrown in the trash!] Whereas in a public library or a school or university library, there is a reason for the library to be there which has nothing to do with problem solving and decision making; what drives the special library is performing to the depth of the requirements of managements. That's really the only reason it's there."

The Need for Case Studies

Wasserman thinks that what means something to management are successful case studies that show how librarians have made a difference in the corporation, not volumes of statistics and circulation numbers. "The case studies should be tied to organizational purpose and speak in ways to the central significance of the library like nothing else can."

> I don't know of any studies that can be done scientifically, but I do know that where there is an effective special librarian, the demonstration of worth, in important measure, is tied to the librarian showing the management how the library made a difference. And with that it is not simply answering questions, and feeling good about having given people information, but following through and identifying *after the fact* what happened to this. Did the fact or article or book we gave you work toward what you were going to use it for? What did you use it for? Did it relate to a product you developed? Did it relate to an important marketing activity? How did what was contributed by our group facilitate or accelerate what was being done? Those questions and answers become very powerful indicators of the usefulness of libraries, librarians, and information services in organizations. The way management perceives the library is in the way that the librarians save time and contribute to and understand the nature of the problem-solving requirements of the people who are doing the work. [Case studies are provided in For More Information.]

Wasserman says that this is very well and widely understood in the context of special librarianship, but it's not so much the case in the academic library or the public library. While he can't say that universally it's ignored, he says there isn't the same premium of concern on the way information can make the difference.

> In the context of the business world an effective special librarian can do much more than simply delivering a fact or an address or biographical sketch. The effective librarian can bring to bear upon certain problems of the organization a whole array of information that has importance and can be put to very fruitful use by problems solvers and decision makers. Historically, management doesn't have enough confidence or faith in librarians to want to delegate more to them than the delivery of an isolated answer to a question.

Learning to Speak the
Language of Business

"If librarians are going to be worth their cost, they need to be able to understand and communicate with the people they serve," says Wasserman.

> Otherwise they're not valuable. Unless they can use the language and logic of the business community, they're forever relegated to being the person who can find the red book, because they don't know what's *in* the red book. We have to evolve occupationally as librarians in special kinds of situations. Librarians who have background and understanding in what they're researching will be in the loop and a wonderful asset.

The Intensive Course on
Business Skills for Librarians

To help train the librarians of the future to be more responsive to the wants and needs of the business community, Wasserman has run an intensive three-week seminar every year entitled "Business Information Services." That course is now taught by someone else within the library school since his retirement. (See Course Outline and Purpose in For More Information.) "We don't usually have students who bring with them a substantial understanding of business and economics here at the library school," he explains. "In the business seminar we focus on the kinds of things that are appropriate to a business administrative context, and we help orient the students to that world of business and economics."

To that end, students in this seminar learn to read a profit/loss balance sheet, to work with business-oriented information resources, and to get a solid grounding in the laws, statistics, institutions, and agencies that are the lifeblood of the typical American corporation. Invited guests from the real world give students the perspective they need to make sense of big business; speakers often include members of the banking industry, the Treasury Department, and the Securities and Exchange Commission. "Being close to Washington, DC is an asset," says Wasserman.

"The student should come out of this seminar with a basic understanding of the business world. The redeeming value of business information is that it's not in a language that's impossible for the lay person to understand. Unlike scientific language, you can learn a lot about business by osmosis if you keep your eyes open and listen," he says.

The Bottom Line

The bottom line is that despite the proliferation of new technologies, Wasserman sees library science as an adaptable field that's more important now than ever. "The point of the librarian is to be the time-saver and the efficient nexus of information," he says. "Why do company managers have to be information literate if they have people who are attuned to their requirements and can get what they need to them swiftly and intelligently?

On His Retirement

At his retirement party in 1995, Paul Wasserman was presented with a gift by his colleagues—one of utmost significance to him and to the library school community: It was a wooden drawer from the school library card catalog, and in the card catalog were the original 20 cards listing the books that contained Wasserman's visions of libraries of the future.

Even though he is officially retired now, he still keeps an office in the library school. In fact, he is still involved in various programs and projects. One of particular importance, in which he is principal investigator, is for a $100,000 pilot program funded by the W. K. Kellogg Foundation (see page 6 for description and homepage) that will link the faculty of Maryland's College of Library and Information Services with the Montgomery County (Maryland) Public Library staff, in a collaborative effort to conduct an economic and community survey and to use the results to begin to build an electronic database on the characteristics of the community. It is hoped that the database growing out of this effort will serve as the beginning of a current inventory of the facts and figures about several of the region's informational characteristics and be designed for regular and continuous updating. The effort is explained in an article written by Wasserman in a librarianship journal:

The project builds on a perceived acute community information requirement, and, through exploiting the professional know-how of the occupation, takes the initiative in inventing and designing an information product and service to meet the requirement. The effort focuses during this pilot phase upon three salient aspects of the county:

- The Environment: such as contains environmental policies and regulations affecting operating businesses in the county
- Quality of Life: includes inventories of characteristics of the region that would be of interest to potential new business and employees moving to the area such as climatic conditions, transportation, election and voting, educational programs, and facilities and health matters
- Business and Economic Concerns; focuses on details about business by category, employment data, organizations supporting business efforts, and related facts[3]

The Kellogg Project is in keeping with Wasserman's focus on creating a new library education paradigm that would provide the following results:

Newly generated purposeful intelligence delivered by the library would offer concrete evidence of the library's civic importance, as well as affording the faculty and student a practical operating base for influencing public library service delivery.[4]

In his article, Wasserman defines the goals of the project (and one of his lifelong visions for the future of education in libraries and librarianship):[5]

Library education faces the imperative to transform itself in fundamental ways to adapt to a culture growing ever more dependent upon technology and information. Simply preparing students to use technology in support of existing activities, such as reference and technical services, neglects the contemporary requisite of equipping students to invent information products and sources required by their clienteles. Education also seeks to foster enhanced teamwork and resource sharing strategies which build on interpersonal collaboration and inter-institutional cooperation. And in the face of the swift pace of present day change, education holds an additional responsibility to lead in continuing educational efforts addressed to the career-long requirements of information specialists.[6]

Notes

1.   Paul Wasserman, *The New Librarianship, A Challenge for Change* (New York: R. R. Bowker, 1972).
2.   Paul Wasserman's *Encyclopedia of Business Information Sources* is available in its 10th edition through Gale Research at 1-800-457-GALE.
3.   Eileen Abels, Gary Marchionini, Paul Wasserman, "A Prospective Alternative Direction for Educational Practice: A Conceptual and Operational Model," *Journal of Education for Library and Information Science* 38 (Summer 1997): 211-214.
4.   Ibid, 211.
5.   Ibid, 213.
6.   Ibid, 214.

For More Information

I.   Additional Q&A between Mary Park and Paul Wasserman

MP: One of the questions that is frequently asked by corporate librarians is, "How do you gain the trust and confidence of the CEO or top managers?" For example, if you work in a larger company where you are several layers down, you can't know the strategic information needs of the CEO, or if you do, you can't always make it known that you do. If you could get the "ear" of the CEO, you might help focus on critical information that is being missed. But the librarian isn't generally perceived as a significant strategic asset in the organization or corporation. That makes it even harder to show how the services of the library can make a difference.

PW: I think the only way to do that is by demonstrated contributions to the organizational purpose. It's not simply a matter of making claims or public relations or rhetorical expressions of how valuable you are, but rather library, as there is demonstration that the librarian or library is committed to getting the job done effectively and swiftly, the organization is put on notice that this is the way things work. When that happens, the librarian has more entree to people in the organization and with that comes a growing understanding of what happens in the organization. For example, in casual discussions with people, simply by learning what people are working on, there can be the proffering of intelligence, information, data which bears upon what people are working on without being asked. I think this has always been the genuine measure of the special librarian. How much are you in tune with who's doing what and who's committed to which problem. It isn't necessarily that they will come and ask directly for information on the problem, but if you are wired into the organizations's workings, and are sensitive to what it's all about and who's working on different things, then the special librarian, knowing what's coming through, what's available, simply matches it up. We have a fancy name for it. We call it SDI (Selective Dissemination of Information), but it really is a correlation between the mind-set of the people doing the work and the librarian who understands what they are doing, comparing what's available and making it accessible to them without being asked for it.

MP: Do you think software can perform the SDI?

PW: Well maybe it will be possible to work out such strategies, but for the foreseeable future it's hard for me to imagine anything that substitutes for the logical mind-set, the intuitive and the sensitive understanding and perception of what people require.

MP: Is it the library school's job to train students and provide them with specialized skills and knowledge, or do you think that this will have to be learned in the context of their work environment?

PW: That's a very good question. I think where we are is that
         we are very, very strongly disposed to ensure that our
         students and our alumni go out with experience,
         understanding, and background in ways to exploit the
         technology so that people are comfortable doing
         searching and people are able to work with the evolving
         technology that is being put in place for resolving
         information needs. The point that is not working as well
         is ensuring that people have a better grounding in the
         substantive material. And it's very hard to do unless
         students come into the college with some kind of
         experience or academic preparation in business because
         we can't, in the course of a library education, equip
         people to be librarians and also equip them to be subject
         specialists. So that's got to come in some other way.
         Now, more and more, some people in librarianship are
         coupling library preparation with some kind of subject
         expertise. For example, it is more common in law
         libraries to find people who not only have library
         preparation, but also focus on legal studies, and that's a
         very powerful combination.

MP: You mentioned paradigm shifts and change agents in
         your book back in the seventies. Where do you think we
         are now in the paradigm shift?

PW: I think we are very far along. It was the case not so many
         years ago (and still in some cases) that we were fixed on
         the idea of the independent, separate library and that the
         library was simply a collection of books. Those notions
         have been scrapped. Even internationally, although it's
         harder to change, there is universal recognition that no
         library stands alone; it can't because it doesn't have the
         resources, it has mutual dependencies. So a freestanding
         library idea is out the window. The collections are
         becoming less and less important; it's really the informa-
         tion sought which is crucial, and so instead of a focus on
         the collection, it shifts to the people and what their needs
         are and how to solve their problems. If I had said this to

you in the seventies, it would have been a revolutionary way of seeing the world, but I think everyone accepts this now, at least theoretically. I think the world understands the difference between what was before and what is now, although the conventions and age-old ways of doing things still exist. In many libraries, for example, if I went to a public library with an information requirement, I would get the reference librarian to try to help me. He/she would work with the existing collection and maybe with the electronic capabilities in the library, not in terms of my problem and how to deal with my problem, but in terms of something that is published or in the library's collection.

In this example it could be that the problem can be resolved more efficiently by just asking an authority or specialist in the subject rather than using the library's resources. But in many places (especially in public libraries), it's not possible for the librarian to make long-distance telephone calls to talk to a specialist in Washington or Chicago. It's not in the budget. So the idea that you solve the problem is still constrained by print, and a whole host of opportunities is cut off because there are restrictions and limitations on how you move the question which has to do with the history, the conventions, and the traditions of librarianship. In this case, we may actually have less expenditure if we go right to where we need to go, i.e., the source of the expertise.

Many librarians tend to put a high level of expectation and faith in the printed material and if one piece of print is good, in librarianship, over five is even better. It keeps the librarian from discriminating. Many times people who want information, at least for certain purposes, want an answer. They don't want half a dozen alternatives. It's as if you went to a doctor who said, "here are five different ways we can deal with your problem and you decide which of them suits you." You would not be very comfortable with that practitioner responding to your

> problem that way, but in libraries that's the way they do. They proffer multiple printed materials and let the client (patron) choose.

MP: Are you implying that if you are doing a job for a CEO that they want to be spoon-fed their information?

PW: Any busy person wants to be spoon-fed. It's answers they are looking for, not a lot of options.

MP: In terms of a paradigm shift, you think we are pretty far along since the seventies?

PW: Clearly.

MP: Where do you think we are going with this?

PW: The ball is too murky. It's very difficult to forecast.

II.   Business Information Services Seminar at The College of Library & Information Services at the University of Maryland: Course Purpose and Outline

Course Purpose:
- To analyze and seek to understand governmental, corporate, and research-based information systems as tools of informed decision making.
- To relate such resources through problem-solving exercises to real-world situations and needs of individuals, institutions, public agencies, and clients of information services.
- To equip the interested person with the perspective and pragmatic skills to serve as an effective information agent of those who require accurate intelligence in the context of interdisciplinary sources, but with particular attention to social, political, and economic considerations.

Course Outline:
  I.   Introduction: Objectives and Procedures
 II.   Governments as Information Sources
III.   Legislation and Regulation
 IV.   Specialized Services in Business and Public Affairs

III. Case Studies of Successful Corporate Libraries and Librarians

1.   These two short cases illustrate the value and impact on the corporation as measured by the benefit of the information professional to the parent organization. One study provides examples taken from corporate information centers' testimonies, *The President's Task Force on the Value of the Information Professional, a Final Report* (Washington, DC: Special Libraries Association, 1987):

- A manufacturing company was sued by an individual claiming that the company had stolen his "secret formula" for a product that the company had just marketed. An information scientist on the staff of the company's technical library found a reference in the technical literature that this formula was generally known to the trade long before the litigant developed his secret formula. When presented with this fact, the litigant dropped his $7 million claim.

- The technical librarian for an electronics firm was asked to do a literature search for one of its engineers. During the course of the search interview, the engineer mentioned that four people had been working to resolve the problem at hand for more than a year. The technical librarian conducted a literature search and found an article that contained the answer the engineer needed to solve his problem, which had been published several years before the time when the project team had begun its work. Had the engineer consulted the technical librarian when the problem was first identified, the company could

have saved four man-years of labor with its resulting
direct monetary costs.

2.   Another study, *The Impact of the Special Library on Corporate
     Decision-Making*, by Joanne G. Marshall for the Special
     Libraries Association in 1993, presents information studies that
     describe examples of the impact of special libraries (business
     and finance libraries) from the corporate decision maker's
     viewpoint:

   - At issue was the possibility of financing a major
     transaction with a forest products company that had
     European subsidiaries. As part of our decision-making
     process we needed to gain a thorough understanding of
     European pulp and paper markets. Library research
     provided us with significant information on European
     markets in general, as well as competitive intelligence.
     We were thus able to make an accurate valuation of
     European assets, which in turn led to a strategic decision.

   - Last week I received a cheque for $7.5M as a
     commitment fee on our proposal to provide financing for
     a management buyout. In addition to this, we will receive
     a $20M closing fee. We were successful in obtaining this
     new business because we were able to demonstrate to the
     principals involved that we understood their industry,
     their markets, and consequently, their financing
     requirements. Your people (library/information centre
     staff) provided the information that enabled us to better
     understand these issues.

   - I was assigned to write a plenary address speech for the
     chairman of xyz for the annual conference of xyz, a
     national organization. I had to familiarize myself quite
     quickly with a range of subjects in auditing, accounting,
     and management relations that I knew very little about.
     To do this I asked the librarians at the [library/informa-
     tion centre] if they could search for books and articles on
     these and other related issues. Within a few days of my
     request, I received a large folder containing the material
     I needed.

I was very impressed not only with the speed but also with the thoroughness and attention to detail with which my request was handled and the material I was supplied, which gave me the background information I needed to write the speech and to develop some of its key points within the confines of my deadline.

By all accounts the speech was a success. A number of business people and government officials have requested copies of the speech. Parts of it were reprinted in the news. I attribute much of the speech's success to the prompt and professional efforts of the staff at the [library/information centre]. Without them, I would not have had the time or the material to do justice to a topic that, at the early stages of my research, was both complex and unfamiliar.

Epilogue

Connectivity, connectivity, ho!
What to do? Where to go?

Mary Woodfill Park

Info Think: Practical Strategies for Using Information in Business was conceived as a way to provide a window on the complexities of the rapidly evolving information environment in the workplace and on the prevailing way people think about and use information in business.

When it was about half finished, the then current thinking began to shift with the surprisingly rapid emergence of the Internet and the World Wide Web, creating their own kind of confusion and chaos. Changing technologies and rapidly growing information resources gave me cause for serious thought about continuing the book. Each time I finished an interview, made the information "current," or added a relevant information resource, things changed.

I resolved, however, that I had gone too far to stop, so I continued to conduct my interviews in the eye of the storm. And I thought of several quotations that served as a reminder of why I wanted to write the book in the first place and why I wanted to stay with it.

One quote came from a 1995 issue of *Science*:

> In the late 1860s Abraham Lincoln's Commissioner of Patents recommended that he plan to close the Commission in a few years. The reason: the rate of discovery had become so great that everything that needed to be discovered would have been discovered by then. The Patent Commission would have no business.

The thought helped me maintain my perspective on just how far we have come since the 1860s, with a discovery rate accelerating at a pace that no one imagined possible. By the late 1990s, we have so much new information and knowledge that we are all overwhelmed by it, and there is a chance it could be devalued or lost if we don't better understand it and develop workable methodologies for finding, using, and preserving it.

It is my belief (my personal infothink) that people can control their own destinies, even in small ways, by knowing, by making themselves more informed personally and professionally about the world and others around them, and by informing and teaching others. This requires responsibility on the part of each individual and a commitment to get to the truth and to the forces behind issues that are potentially dangerous, troublesome, or promising. The choices for those who aren't well informed (for whatever reasons) can be disastrous. Wars have been won and lost, people have suffered and died, and companies have failed because information has been burned, controlled, manipulated, lost, deleted, ignored, or disregarded. Examples are everywhere.

Now is not the time to ignore or forget the lessons we have learned from these examples. Nor is it time to forget who we are. Mankind has come so far in creating knowledge, in organizing, preserving, and making it available through its libraries and now through electronic access.

Now is the time to become even more alert to its safekeeping and use, keeping in mind at all times the inherent and potential dangers of making so much information available to mankind without providing the methodologies and skills to use it.

During the writing of *InfoThink*, I must admit that I have sometimes felt like Sisyphus—overwhelmed, dreaming that the big boulder was about to overcome me because I could not keep up with the information. In fact, in the earlier days of the Internet, I read something that also had an impact on why I was continuing to write. In 1994, Joel Achenbach wrote in *The Washington Post Magazine*: "The information counter-revolution is the next great step. There will be a push to get unwired. A lust for silence."

I have been tempted to succumb to this notion. But I now believe that that thought will increasingly become unthinkable, particularly in business environments. We will have to handle larger amounts of data and information, to become multifaceted, multidimensional, to exercise greater intelligence, to tolerate more vagueness, to become more articulate in what we need to communicate, because we will all be governed by the need to make sense of our environment and to do so quickly.

We are all becoming knowledge workers. In our offices of the future, we will be founding, forging, and manufacturing information in many forms and of many materials. Whether we are successful, articulate information creators and users will depend on whether we can develop the conceptual tools in time to avoid the great floods of information coming our way, and on whether we make use of what concepts and skills already exist. Neglecting these issues will create an information incompetent society where we will become slaves like Sisyphus. As Peter Drucker once said, "We have an enormous job ahead of us, making ourselves and our businesses information literate."

In closing, I believe that these tasks ahead of us may seem more than daunting, but as we near the turn of the century, we could be the creators of another of mankind's greater moments—if we can meet the challenges upon us.

Index

About the Author

Mary Woodfill Park has over 25 years of research and management experience in corporate, academic, and public libraries and information centers. In 1987 she founded her own company, The Information Consultancy, to help meet the business information needs of companies and individuals. Ms. Park has been an active participant in numerous associations and organizations representing the information industry and the library/information services profession, including Special Libraries Association (SLA), American Society for Information Science (ASIS), Association of Independent Information Professionals (AIIP), Society of Competitive Intelligence Professionals (SCIP), and The Information Futures Institute. She has written about many information topics in her newsletter, *InfoProse. The Newsletter from the Information Professionals©*, and is a frequent speaker on the topic of "The Information Literate Executive." Ms. Park is listed in *Who's Who in America* and Harvard Business School's *International Directory of Business and Management Scholars and Research* and was named one of "Maryland's Top 100 Women" by *Warfield's Business Record*. She lives in Baltimore and enjoys hiking and fishing with her family in the Rocky Mountains of Montana.